"YUP."

"NOPE."

"MAYBE"

A WOMAN
TO GETTING MORE
THE LANGUAGE OF MEN

Tyndale House Publishers, Inc.
Carol Stream, Illinois

STEPHEN JAMES
DAVID THOMAS

Visit Tyndale's exciting Web site at www.tyndale.com

TYNDALE and Tyndale's quill logo are registered trademarks of Tyndale House Publishers, Inc.

"Yup." "Nope." "Maybe.": A Woman's Guide to Getting More out of the Language of Men

Designed by Jacqueline L. Noe

Edited by Dave Lindstedt

Published in association with the literary agency of Baugher & Co., 611 Eastcastle Court, Franklin, TN 37069.

Library of Congress Cataloging-in-Publication Data

James, Stephen, date.
  "Yup." "nope." "maybe." : a woman's guide to getting more out of the language of men / Stephen James and David Thomas.
     p. cm.
  Includes bibliographical references.
  ISBN-13: 978-1-4143-1207-1 (sc)
  ISBN-10: 1-4143-1207-5 (sc)
  1. Marriage—Religious aspects—Christianity. 2. Communication in marriage. 3. Interpersonal relations—Religious aspects—Christianity. I. Thomas, David, date. II. Title.
  BV835.J35 2007
  248.8′44—dc22   2006034986

Printed in the United States of America

13   12   11   10   09   08   07
 7   6   5   4   3   2   1

CONTENTS

Acknowledgments V

Introduction: Are guys as clueless as they act? VII

1 "YUP. NOPE. MAYBE." 1
(Decoding manspeak)

2 "I'M NOT LOST." 13
(Why won't men stop for directions?)

3 "IN A MINUTE." 27
(Why do men spend so much time on the toilet?)

4 "CAN'T IT WAIT TILL HALFTIME?" 45
(What's the deal with guys and sports?)

5 "WANNA DO IT?" 65
(Do men *always* think about sex?)

6 "YOUR PROBLEM IS . . ." 87
(Why does he always try to fix my problems?)

7 "YOU'RE TOO SENSITIVE!" 111
(Are men just emotionally constipated?)

8 "WHAT WERE YOU THINKING?" 135
(Why women will always have questions about men.)

9 CONCLUSION 145

Conversation Starters 147

Notes 155

About the Authors 159

"YUP."
"NOPE."
"MAYBE."

A WOMAN'S GUIDE
TO GETTING MORE OUT OF
THE LANGUAGE OF MEN

STEPHEN JAMES
DAVID THOMAS

THIS BOOK MADE ME *LAUGH!*

More than that, it gave me so much insight into the way my husband thinks and how I could possibly communicate better. Men and women alike will relate to and enjoy this book. It's an easy, fun read that you'll tell your friends about. I loved it.

SINGER/SONGWRITER **CINDY MORGAN**

THIS BOOK IS A MUST-READ FOR WOMEN.

James and Thomas offer invaluable insight into the mysterious world of men and why they make us crazy.

CARA DAVIS, EDITORIAL DIRECTOR, *RELEVANT* MAGAZINE; EDITOR *RADIANT* MAGAZINE

ACKNOWLEDGMENTS

BETWEEN THE TWO OF US, we have seven kids (four for Stephen and three for David). And better than that, surprisingly, we both have a set of twin boys. Neither one discovered we were having twins until midway through our wives' pregnancies. Needless to say, we were shocked. There's something uniquely challenging about birthing and raising multiples. We were equally shocked when Tyndale approached us with the idea of simultaneously birthing two books, *"Yup." "Nope." "Maybe."* and *"Does This Dress Make Me Look Fat?"*

The process of creating books is somewhat akin to pregnancy. You gain a lot of weight. (We each usually sock on ten to twenty pounds as we eat our way through a manuscript.) There is a good deal of waiting. (The entire writing/publishing process took more than eighteen months). And there is a whole lot of labor that you're not sure will ever end. (Only about one-third of what we wrote made the final manuscript.) Then all of a sudden, your labor brings forth something. And as birth goes, it's usually more complicated when birthing multiples—which was certainly the case for our twins (all three sets).

One other similarity to pregnancy is that you can't make books on your own. You've gotta have help—and the better the support, the more positive the delivery experience. We had the best folks attending to us than anyone could ever hope to have.

Thanks to the entire crew at Tyndale for their encouragement, professionalism, and effort. Working with you all is nothing short of fantastic. Thanks especially to Ken Petersen and Carol Traver for investing deeply in two goobers from Tennessee and believing that depth and humor aren't mutually exclusive. Deep gratitude is also owed to Dave Lindstedt, our fearless editor, whose firm but gentle hand made everything you read . . . well, readable.

We must also thank our remarkable agent, Matt Baugher. We both well remember leaving his office after our first introduction, looking at each other and saying, "We gotta work with that guy." Matt, you are excellent at what you do. Thanks for representing us so well, for being so diplomatic, and for rounding off a lot of our rough edges. It is an honor to know you and to work alongside you.

Heather and Connie, our supportive wives. We *know* the two of you have asked, "Why did I sign on for this?" And the fact that you put up with us, and our frequent absences while writing, is humbling. There really aren't words to acknowledge your sacrifice—and we don't even pretend to understand.

We are continuously awed by God's grace and his profound sense of humor. That he would entrust us the opportunity to write of his mystery and magnificence is baffling and humbling. If you discover anything more of his love and mercy in these pages, it is indeed a miracle.

Stephen and David

WHY ANOTHER BOOK on women and men? That's a great question. It all started one evening last summer, when I (Stephen) was watching TV with my wife. It was warm in the house, so I got up and adjusted the thermostat to cool off. "Are you hot?" she asked. "Because I am freezing." A few minutes later, she got up to get a glass of water. I noticed that as she passed the thermostat, she adjusted it back to where it had been. Now, I should have left it alone, but because I'm a man, I couldn't let it go. Consequently, a silent battle began over the thermostat—just a little unspoken conflict fought with stealthy maneuvers and cunning strategy. The thermostat bounced back and forth all night, and we both lost the war. I stayed hot and she stayed cold.

In an effort to strike a peace accord and thus restore harmony to the atmospheric condition of my home, I asked a mechanical-engineer friend who designs heating and cooling systems to help me out. He explained it this way: "Heat dissipation is a function of surface area (r^2), and heat production is a function of volume (r^3); so the production-to-dissipation ratio corresponds with the radius."

"Huh?" I asked with an expression that looked like I had just ingested a mouthful of bad cottage cheese.

"The smaller you are, the colder you'll be."

This got me thinking, and I decided to do some research. I learned that because women menstruate, they are more prone to anemia, which can make them feel cold. I also discovered that a woman's core body temperature varies little, in order to provide a healthier growing environment for babies in utero. Consequently, if a woman's core temperature drops by a little bit, all the blood gets drawn from the extremities into the core. When a man's core temperature drops by a little bit, it just sits there, no problem. This all made sense, and it explained why even in the summer my petite wife has been known to turn on the in-seat heater when she is in the car.

I recounted this skirmish to David, my friend and cowriter, over a cup of coffee one day, and he asked, "Why would God make men and women so completely different and then call us to share life together, to be in intimate relationship with one another? It seems like the opportunities for conflict and misunderstanding are enormous. Is God crazy? I wish some guys would write a book that explained to women what men are really thinking."

"Hey, that's a great idea, David."

As we did the research for this book, we were reminded of many things we had learned in grad school. For instance, that there are basic biological differences between men and women. These differences are easily recognizable when we consider the structure of male and female brains and our differing physiologies. For example, the male brain has greater hemispheric separation, which helps to explain why men have a skill for abstract reasoning and visual-spatial intelligence (and why more men are engineers). The female brain has more frequent interactions and larger connections between the left and right hemispheres, which can explain why women are generally more skilled in verbal and written expression, have a stronger mastery of language, and possess the marks of intuition and empathy (and why more women are counselors).

Poet Robert Bly describes the female brain as a "superhighway" of connection, whereas the connections in the male brain are better described as a "little crookedy country road." Perhaps, like us, you are curious about why we are invited to travel the superhighway and the little crookedy country road together.

THE BIG DEAL OF SEX

Sexuality directly and significantly influences almost every aspect of our lives. Femaleness or maleness is hardwired into our physiology, anthropology, and theology—it's written into our hearts, minds, souls, and bodies. We're aware of sexuality from a very early age. Children discern the difference in the sexes before they ever notice other variations like height, ethnicity, or hair color.

This idea that sex is central to our lives is neither new nor particularly profound. We all pretty much know how pervasive it is. Take a look around. Our culture is laden with sexual images, sexual stereotypes, and sexual innuendos. From high art to beer commercials, sexuality is the common lexicon.

Sex is ubiquitous. Just visit the supermarket. You can't even buy a bag of groceries without being inundated with sexuality. Next time you're in the checkout aisle, take a look at the magazines: *Cosmo, People, Us, Entertainment Weekly.* Sex is everywhere. Heck, it's even in the pages of *Wired,* an award-winning science and technology magazine I (Stephen) subscribe to. In one issue, there was a big, yellow, eye-catching bubble on the cover that read, "Women, Sex, and the Science of Orgasm."[1] This teaser heralded an article exploring the scientific search to create female Viagra. (No need to speculate. Of course I read that article first.)

All this attention on sex is not part of a vast left-wing conspiracy (despite what Rush Limbaugh might say). Sex is everywhere for one simple reason: It's central to our human experience. Sex *sells* because advertisers know that it scratches an elemental itch at the core of who we are. Even the Bible makes a big deal about sexuality, tying it to spirituality and intimacy with God.

THE DUDE AND THE GIRL

About the same time we started talking about this book, I (David) began premarital counseling with a couple who lived in two different cities. I met with them on weekends when the groom-to-be was in town. He was, as they say, a man of very few words. A woman might say he was "emotionally constipated." We'll refer to him simply as Dude Can't Talk.

The bride-to-be was quite verbal (if you can imagine that). We'll refer to her affectionately as Girl Won't Shut Up. Because of their long-distance relationship, her desire was for them to speak by phone at the end of each day, simply to "hear each other's voice." Dude Can't Talk obliged her with this nightly ritual, but things did not go as planned.

According to Girl Won't Shut Up, they would chat freely for ten to fifteen minutes. That of course was the part of the conversation where she talked about her day. What she'd eaten for breakfast. What route she'd driven to work. How relationships at work were progressing. The errands she'd run after work. Whom she had talked to on the phone that day, and when. What her mother had said about the people she had talked to on the phone that day. Making sure he knew that Brad and Angelina were expecting. How her training for the half-marathon was going. And discussing their plans for the next weekend he would be in town.

Dude Can't Talk would throw in an occasional "yup," "nope," or "maybe," and every once in a while, he would follow it with an "uh-huh."

The next portion of the evening chat often involved a good deal of silence. According to Dude Can't Talk, he wondered to himself, *Why in the world do we stay on the line if there is nothing left to say?* One night, tired from a day of making sales calls, he mustered up enough courage to say, "This is silly. We should just finish the conversation if we're done talking."

Girl Won't Shut Up, in her desperation to create some kind of connection, brought this up at our next counseling session, saying to Dude Can't Talk, "I'd rather hear you breathing on the other end of the line than not hear you at all."

This comment was greeted with silence by Dude Can't Talk.

Girl Won't Shut Up then vowed not to carry so much of the conversation from this point on. She had come to the conclusion that she was doing too much work in their relationship, and this was just one example. Her solution was to wait patiently for Dude Can't Talk to take the lead in their phone dialogue. This would be his way of proving his interest in her, in the relationship, and in communication.

I remember thinking, *I can't wait to see how this turns out.*

When the couple arrived for their next weekend session, I asked how the new strategy was working. Girl Won't Shut Up reported that the first nightly phone call after our last meeting began as they always had, with her description of her day's activities, and an exchange of logistical information. But then she remembered her now-sacred vow of silence.

"I just stayed silent . . . for what felt like five minutes or more, until . . . until . . ."

Until she just couldn't take it anymore.

According to Dude Can't Talk, at this point she yelled, "Well, at least tell me what you're wearing right now! Do you even know how to have a conversation?"

Girl Won't Shut Up looked away as he tattled on her, but then she shifted toward me, still full of energy, and said, "Answer me this, 'Dr. Phil.' Is he really as clueless as he acts? I wish some man would write a book for women explaining what is going on inside a guy's head."

I thought to myself, *Now that you mention it . . .*

"MANSPEAK"

Dude Can't Talk and Girl Won't Shut Up are extreme examples, in some ways, but their relationship illustrates one aspect of how differences in men and women affect their relational intimacy and authenticity. When two guys are having a heart-to-heart, a lot can be communicated with a few head nods, a couple of grunts, and the occasional, well-chosen expletive. But from a woman's perspective, men aren't quite so clear. What a woman *hears* a man say, what he *doesn't* say, and what he's *trying* to say are very often disconnected. Here are a few examples:

A woman asks a man, "Are you happy in our relationship?" He says, "Yup." She hears, "He's not that into me," but he might really mean, "I've never been happier."

At the end of a very romantic and connected day, the man

says something like, "Wanna do it?" She more than likely thinks, *All he wants is sex. That* Pig! What he meant was, "I really love you and want to make love with you."

A woman comes home from a really disappointing day at the office and unloads her frustration about her boss and coworkers on her husband, crying the entire time. He responds with, "What you need to do is . . ." Feeling dismissed and lonely, she leaves the room and calls her mother. What he was trying to say was, "It scares me that I don't believe that I am enough for you right now."

One lazy Sunday afternoon, a wife says to her husband, "I need to talk to you about John Jr. and the note his teacher sent home from school." He says, "Can't it wait until halftime?" Her interpretation: "He doesn't love our son." What he was thinking was, *I have no idea what to do.*

With men and women (as with so much of life) what you see is not always what you get. It's a lot more complicated than men and women being from different planets or just needing love or respect. The trouble is that we are very similar in substance but different enough in form and structure that unless we are intentional in listening and interpreting each other well, we will miss the mark, even though we are often after the same things.

TWENTY QUESTIONS

One of the best parts of writing this book was the research. We began by sending out a mass e-mail to every woman we knew, explaining the concept of this book and requesting that they send us questions they had about men—things that bewildered them, things that caused them great frustration, and things that they just wanted to know more about. We got hundreds of replies from women from all over the country, and a wide variety of questions, such as these:

- Why won't men stop to ask for directions?
- Are men just emotionally constipated?
- Do men *always* think about sex?
- How can men fight fearlessly in war and yet whimper like children when they're sick?
- Why are some men afraid to get married?
- Why do men spend so much time on the porcelain throne?
- What frightens men about becoming fathers?
- Why can't men ever find what they're looking for?
- Why do men leave their socks and shoes on the floor?
- Why don't men help with the children the way their wives would like?
- Why do men watch sports?
- Why do men like gadgets?
- Why do men drive fast?

Once we had received all these questions, we reviewed them for similarities and common themes. We then set up dinners with women of various ages, races, and socioeconomic backgrounds. Some were married; others were single. Some were grandmothers; others were barely out of their teens. Some had children; others did not.

We asked these women to tell us all the questions they had about men—and they did, talking for hours. We took great notes, we laughed (and laughed some more), and often we scratched our heads. These questions opened the door to extraordinary conversations, which became the foundation for this book. Our method was far from scientific, but it sure was fun. In the end, what we learned is that women really don't understand all that much about men, and they have many more questions than answers.

When we sat down to write, one thing was certain: It was going to be a book about sex. Not about the act of sexual intercourse but the energy created by the differences between men and women. This book, as honestly as possible, explores the inner dynamics of men and women in relationship. It's a book that looks deeply into the hearts of each gender and exposes something true and hopeful about what is at play between the sexes.

We came to the conclusion that men are in no way as clueless as they sometimes act. However, we do believe that the demand placed on men, in an increasingly feminized culture, to *relate like women* is dangerous. We're also certain that many men are emotionally and relationally stunted, and we observed that women and men both use the excuse "Hey, he's just being a man" as a way to escape the struggle of engaging with members of the opposite sex, who are so different and yet so intriguing.

We hope to accomplish two things with this book: 1) Show women how to move beyond the question of "Is he as clueless as he acts?" to embrace a genuine curiosity and appreciation for the differences in men, so that women can discover acceptance for their own presence, power, and purpose; and 2) inspire men to be as curious about women and begin to see the heart behind their actions, so that their masculinity will more likely be authentic, safe, courageous, and full.

Men and women are each God's image-bearers. We all

have the same core feelings, needs, desires, longings, and hopes. Women and men were both created as relational beings by a relational God in a relational context. But how we engage with that context, navigate relationships, and interpret data are vastly different. Most of these differences are rooted in our gender.

God's hope for sexuality is far grander and more glorious than the lewd, prurient, lustful presentations that dominate so much of our culture. If you want to understand life and live well, love well, and parent well, then you need to understand a fundamental ingredient of our humanity—sexuality, and how it interacts with and influences all other areas of life.

Have fun.

1
"YUP. NOPE. MAYBE."

JAKE AND ANNE were wrestling with the idea of starting a family. They had been married for "four very long years," and Anne was ready to take the jump into parenthood. Jake, on the other hand, was "fine with holding off for a while." Anne was a mover and a shaker, but Jake preferred to take things slow. They had been coming to me (David) for counseling for several months, and helping them work through their decision about children had been a bit like refereeing a friendly game of Twister between Orville Redenbacher and Martha Stewart.

Anne would typically come well-prepared, with notebook in hand, all assignments from the week completed, and a list of additional questions she'd like to ask during our session. Jake, on the other hand, rarely remembered his assignment or had only partially completed it. Anne would shake her head in disbelief, frustration, and sadness, and then Jake would laugh awkwardly and say something like, "I should take better notes when I'm here, shouldn't I?" The conversation would start at medium volume and build to a crescendo of contempt, apologies, and tears.

One evening, when Jake again came unprepared, Anne was running low on forgiveness. Following his usual "aw, shucks" confession, Anne lit into him.

"You're kidding, right?"

"Nope," he replied apologetically, but he was looking at me, not at her.

"What?!" With a single word, Anne captured all the energy and frustration of four years of unmet expectations.

"I forgot," Jake added sheepishly. I thought to myself, *Oh man, you're in trouble now . . . big trouble.*

Anne snapped, "Do you even want to do this?"

Jake, eager to make up for lost ground, put just a little too much enthusiasm into his response: "Yeah!"

(Let me pause here and give you some brief history. During the several months that I had been counseling Anne and Jake, I had given him some questions and statements that he could use anytime he was unsure about how to pursue his wife's heart.)

When Anne's tight lips and narrowed eyes conveyed her doubts about his commitment to the counseling process, Jake began regurgitating every key phrase I had taught him—simultaneously. "What do you need from me?" "Help me understand how I've hurt you." "I want to know your heart, Anne." "How do you feel?" "What you say is important to me!" "Tell me what you need right now!" He paused and racked his brain, like a schoolboy searching for the last phrase in reciting the Preamble to the Constitution.

I gave him a look that said, "Jake, that's more than enough. Just buckle your seatbelt tightly. The car is about to crash."

Anne hung her head, and Jake and I waited in silence. *Here come the tears,* I thought.

When she looked up, her eyes were wet, but her voice was steady. "I want you to get off your butt and do something! Do you hear me talking to you, Jake?"

It was quiet for a long moment, and Jake seemed like he was afraid to move. I adjusted in my seat to get comfortable. Finally, Jake looked at me as if to say, "Help me out here, man. . . . Don't we have some kind of secret man-pact? Can't you see I'm drowning?"

Rather than throw him the life preserver he so desperately wanted, I decided to let him tread water for a while, and I tossed him a question instead. "Jake, do you know what your wife is asking from you?"

"Maybe?" He looked at me helplessly, his expression a mixture of uncertainty and disorientation—like a man who had just been dragged into a bridal shower. Then, realizing he should say more, he added, "Well, obviously to do *something*."

Anne was now crying without reserve.

"And what is that something she is wanting from you?" I asked.

Jake became anxious at this point and started shifting in his seat. "I know where you're headed," he said, pointing his finger at me and then at his wife, "and I've told you I'm not ready for kids yet."

Anne didn't even look up, but I knew her heart was breaking.

"Jake, I don't think she's asking you to conceive *tonight.*

3

But she is aching to know that you are interested in the desires of her heart, the things she wants, even if it scares the life out of you." (And, boy, was he scared.)

"She wants you to chase after her the way you did when you first met . . . to be that interested in her again. And, yes, it may eventually lead you to having a child. And if that's the case, well, you're a smart guy. You'll figure out what to do along the way."

I stopped and looked at Anne again. She had stopped crying and was nodding her head, as if to say, "Preach on, brother." Jake looked trapped, but also a little relieved. Not because he didn't know what to do, but because he knew exactly what to do . . . exactly what was required of him.

I once commented to Jake that he had been given the gift of a passionate woman. Anne is strong, expressive, and engaging. (She can also be demanding, impatient, controlling, and resentful). Like many women, she is hungry to be chosen and led. Jake is an articulate, well-educated, confident man, but like many men I know, he also has a deer-in-the-headlights look that he puts on frequently. (You know the one—a little mild terror mixed with some confusion and a touch of "oh crap.") And there's nothing quite like a relationship with a strong woman to make an otherwise confident man turn into a frightened, shell-shocked, fumbling-his-words little boy. "Yup. Nope. Maybe. I don't know. Maybe. What do you want? Maybe."

CROSS-CULTURAL COMMUNICATION

For a couple of years, I (Stephen) lived in Seattle. My entire life previous to this Northwest stint, I had lived in and around Nashville. I'm a Southerner, born and raised, but I'm no yokel. I don't often say "y'all." At one time or another, I've traveled to most parts of the country and have spent the obligatory summer in Europe. I have an undergraduate degree in English literature, and I know the difference between a split infinitive and a prepositional phrase. I have been told more than once in my life, "You don't sound like you're from the South." But after being in Seattle for only a few weeks, I felt like Gomer Pyle at Tavern on the Green. I hadn't experienced such cultural self-consciousness since my parents moved us to an upscale, preppy suburb when I was in fifth grade, and I showed up for school with a Butt Cut hairstyle, black parachute pants, and a verbal twang that would shame a country-western singer.

One afternoon, my wife, daughter, and I were at a busy Seattle restaurant for lunch. We had been seated for quite some time without having our order taken, so I waved a waiter over to our table. As pleasantly and assertively as I could, I said, "Excuse me. We haven't ordered yet. Can we get some help?"

The waiter just stared at me, slightly bewildered. "Sir?" he asked.

Thinking he must not have heard me, I repeated myself, "Can we get some help?"

There was a long pause as his bewilderment grew into a general confusion. Then very sincerely and apologetically, he leaned toward me and said, "I'm sorry, sir, but I don't think we have 'hep' on the menu. Can I get you something else?"

If two people from different geographical regions (like my waiter friend and me) can speak different dialects of the same language, you can understand how communication between men and women can be equally cross-cultural. After all, we grow up in different worlds biologically, socially, emotionally, and psychologically; and we have distinctly different views of the world as a result. We are creatures of different cultures, with different ideas of what life is all about. Nowhere does this break down more obviously than in our language.

To understand the male culture, we have to understand *manspeak,* because language is at the root of every culture. To comprehend the nuances, components, and character of a particular culture, we must embrace and understand the language. For instance, if we were to say to an English-speaking friend, "It will blow you away," she would know we were referring to something extraordinary. But if we said to a Spanish-speaking friend, "Te soplará ausente" (literally, "It will blow you absent"), our statement would make no sense. If we wanted to communicate effectively, we would have to choose an equivalent Spanish idiom, such as "Te dejará alucinada" (literally, "It will leave you hallucinated"), which makes no sense in English, but which idiomatically communicates the same idea as the English phrase "It will blow you away." The point, of course, is that men *and* women must speak in terms the other will understand if they want to communicate effectively.

With men and women, the nuances are often quite subtle. For example, take the little word *upset.* It's pretty innocuous, right? Wrong. When a woman tells a man, "I'm upset," what does she mean? She is hurt, sad, depressed, lonely. But more than likely what the man hears is, "I'm angry," and he immediately thinks, *What did I do to make her so mad?* He's likely to respond defensively—a far cry from the compassion that the woman was looking for.

Deborah Tannen, in her book *You Just Don't Understand,* labels the differences in the communication styles of women and men as "rapport-talk and report-talk."[1] According to Tannen, women use conversation to maintain intimacy, increase connection, and develop rapport. Men, on the other hand, talk to establish independence, build status, and deliver data. Keep in mind, too, that what is *said* is only a small part of what is communicated. Researchers generally agree that upwards of 70 to 80 percent of all communication is nonverbal. To decode the language of men, you need to open your eyes, not just your ears. For example, when women talk to each other, they stand close together, maintain eye contact, and gesture frequently. Men typically keep a greater distance, avoid eye contact, and gesture much less often. The differences go on and on.

BREAKING THE CODE

I (David) teach a seminar called Nurturing Boys, in which I spend a good deal of time coaching parents and educators on how to crack the "male code." The male code is a not-so-secret, but often misunderstood, language that males use to communicate with the world around them. Composed of single-word responses, grunting, brooding, and a generous measure of silence, the code involves meanings hidden within other meanings and a full range of nonverbal communication. Because teenage boys are especially fluent in this language, their parents must learn how to translate what is being communicated but not necessarily verbalized. For example, "Leave me alone!" the mantra of many a teenage boy, most often means, "I am trying to be independent, but I also feel really scared; and I'm hoping you'll stay close to me."

"You don't understand" means, "Please be interested in me." It is an invitation to pursue and engage with your teenage boy.

At every seminar, so far without exception, a handful of women will approach me to thank me for breaking the code. They will usually say something along the lines of, "This will be helpful with my son, but now I am beginning to really understand my *husband!*"

SEX ON THE BRAIN

Science continues to discover and prove how men's and women's brains really do work differently. Whatever separates the sexes, it all begins with a solitary Y chromosome, which influences, among other things, the size of certain brain structures and how the brain is wired.

Though men typically have bigger heads and larger brains than women, both sexes score equally well on IQ tests. How come? Women have about 15 to 20 percent more gray matter than men—the part of the brain tissue that supplies focused power and the ability to link thoughts.

Men's heads are filled with more white matter and fluid.[2] (No, that is not a joke.) White matter helps to distribute processing power throughout the brain. This gives men better spatial reasoning, which is part of the reason most men prefer to figure out directions rather than ask for them. White matter also allows for single-mindedness, which explains why men tend not to be great multitaskers (and why men are able to tune out everything except the football game).

The white matter in women's brains is concentrated in the corpus callosum (the part of the brain that links its hemispheres).

This helps both sides of the brain talk to each other more easily, which explains why women are more verbally capable than men.

Male and female brains age differently, too. Women have better blood flow to the brain. As men age, they lose more brain tissue, especially in the part of the brain that considers consequences and regulates self-control. (Again, this is not a joke, nor is it an excuse.)

A study by Dr. Peter Silverstone, a psychiatrist at the University of Alberta, shows that men and women use different parts of the brain while completing the same tasks.[3] The study involved volunteers who performed a variety of tasks while their brain activity was monitored by MRI. Silverstone's work reveals how men's and women's brains are fundamentally wired differently. His findings begin to explain why depression, for example, occurs twice as often in women as in men; and why men suffer from schizophrenia, alcoholism, and attention deficit disorder at much greater frequency than women.

Scientific discovery is just beginning to explain some of these differences, and the implications are huge for these lines of research. In the future, we may see medical treatments for men and women evolve to become more gender specific, based on differences in brain composition and structure.

SEX IN THE SOUL

The differences between men and women are far more pervasive than even brain structure, genital design, cultural cues, and biological makeup can explain. There is a deep spiritual significance in how men and women are created that gives further insight into the language that men use—and don't use.

In Genesis, the first book in the Bible, God gives human-ity the responsibility to "fill the earth and subdue it."[4] Adam is placed in the Garden of Eden, and his first job is to name all the animals.[5] The responsibility for naming things is very significant. It comes directly from man's creation in the image of God, and it reflects the character and essence of God, who *spoke* all things into existence.[6] In Genesis 1, God speaks and creates beauty out of nothing and order out of chaos. In Genesis 2, God gives Adam the responsibility for naming every living creature. The ancient Israelites, for whom the book of Genesis was originally written, would have understood that the process of naming the animals not only identified and classified them, but also spoke to their character—the essence of their creatureliness.

In the task he assigned to Adam, God had at least two pur-poses:

1. To let Adam express the image of God in him by utilizing his creativity, his stewardship over the earth, and his deep con-nection to creation.
2. To help Adam recognize his loneliness and his need for a helper "suitable for him"[7]—that is, a creature also created in the image of God. As God says in Genesis 2:18, "It is not good for the man to be alone."

The next thing we know, God is knocking Adam out cold, pulling out one of his ribs, and making a woman (Eve) to rescue Adam from his loneliness. When Adam awakens and sees Eve for the first time, his response is not a simple "Thank you, God," or a tepid "Yup," "Nope," or "Maybe." No, Adam goes way beyond that—he bursts into poetry:

"This is now bone of my bones
    and flesh of my flesh;
she shall be called 'woman,'
    for she was taken out of man."[8]

This is a high point for Adam, and in his joy he *shouts out* his gratitude and awe—the first recorded act of worship.

This story from Genesis, from the very earliest days of man's existence, underscores the tremendous power of words—especially the words of a man—to bring boundaries and order to an unruly world. That is why when a man fails to speak, he passes up the chance to shape his world with the words of his heart. As a result, the shadows of evil darken his life, as well as the lives of those around him.

However, when a man is authentic and speaks out of and in harmony with his design, he profoundly reveals God's glory and his own strength and nobility. Now, the words he speaks may not be as elaborate or voluminous as his female counterpart's, but they don't have to be. If they are true, they will have merit, and their weight will count for good. On the other hand, if he doesn't take ownership of his heart through his words, his words will be weak and disposable, and at best they will warm the air for a moment before dissipating.

Although the differences between men and women provide material for stand-up comics and water cooler jocularity, they don't imply superiority or inferiority for one sex or the other. But insofar as these differences shape our language, and thus spread out into the nooks and crannies of our lives, they have a profound effect on the quality of our relationships.

SO, WHAT'S A WOMAN TO DO?

1. Remember, with men (as with debt and infection), less is more. He may be saying a lot with very few words.
2. Avoid the tendency to read more into the situation than is actually there. Yes, men and boys require some reading between the lines, but avoid the tendency to infuse your own stuff into his meaning.
3. Resist the temptation to speak for him. Too often, women throw out emotional life preservers when men don't need (or want) rescuing.
4. If you find yourself going nuts waiting for his response, just remember what we told you: As men age, they lose more brain tissue. You can always blame it on that.

"I'M NOT LOST."

WHY WON'T MEN STOP FOR DIRECTIONS?

HEATHER AND I (Stephen) had not been married long, maybe a few months, when we decided to go hiking one Saturday afternoon in a nearby park. It was a beautiful fall day. The air was cool and dry, and the leaves were just beginning to change color. As we set off from the parking area up the first hill, we entered the woods and became wrapped in the russet glow of sunlight illuminating the canopy of autumn leaves—oh, so romantic.

As we climbed the first hill hand in hand, Heather reminded me that we were meeting her parents for dinner that evening. We had about four hours to hike a few miles, drive back to our apartment, and get cleaned up before meeting her parents.

Plenty of time, I thought.

With confidence, I led my bride over the first big hill and

down the other side. Within a few minutes, we were on a trail deeper into the woods. As we walked, we talked intently about our growing relationship and our future.

About an hour later, Heather asked, "Don't we need to be heading back soon?"

I reassured her that we had plenty of time and could keep going a little longer before we turned back. So we climbed a few more hills and explored a few more trails.

A little more time passed before Heather politely asked again, "Don't you think we need to be heading back to the car?"

"You're right," I agreed. "It's about that time." It was probably three-thirty in the afternoon, and the sun was just beginning its descent toward the horizon. If I had judged it right, we were about forty-five minutes from the car. Still plenty of time to get home, change, and meet her parents by six.

As we continued our conversation, I led us to the next trail fork, and we turned left onto a path that took us up a steep hill. We walked along the ridgeline for probably another twenty minutes, before I began to wonder where we were.

Should we have gone to the right back there? But I quickly dismissed the idea, and we carried on.

This particular park was fairly large—probably a few hundred acres of woods and fifty-plus miles of intersecting roads, paved hiking paths, and trails that meandered up and down the hills and snaked through the valleys. We had been hiking for a couple of hours now, and I was starting to doubt my sense of where we were. Heather, too, was starting to get nervous. "Do you know where we are?" she asked.

"Yes," I replied, with as much conviction as I could rally.

(This was not altogether a lie. I knew we were in the park, I knew we were on top of a hill . . . and I knew we were lost.)

We walked on a little farther.

"Are you sure you know where we're going?" Heather asked again. This time, there was a touch more accusation than question in her voice.

"Yeah, it's this way," I bluffed, but my façade was beginning to crack. (I know what you're thinking: *What a joker.* But hey, it's not like she asked, "How do we get back to the car?")

"Stephen!" She had stopped walking and was insistent now. "How do we get back to the car?"

At this point, any wise man would have admitted he didn't have a clue. (Heck, any wise man would have grabbed a map back at the parking area on his way in to the park.) Well . . . I'm not just *any* wise man, so instead I replied indignantly, "Heather! Don't you trust me? Come on, it's this way."

I must have sounded pretty convincing, because for the next hour, she followed me all over the park, not saying a word while I searched for any familiar log, rock, or road that would lead us out.

By now, dusk had settled in, and the light was fading in the treetops. The sky had turned gray, and as we headed down yet another hill, it began to sprinkle. Heather's parents would be arriving at the restaurant soon (I think it was about a quarter to six). We, on the other hand, would not be. I was seriously beginning to wonder whether we would make it out at all. By the look on Heather's face, she was sharing my doubts. And then, just like that, we walked around a bend in the trail and saw a sign directing us to the parking area.

15

Within five minutes, we were in the car heading home. Heather called her parents on the cell phone to tell them we would be late. She hates being late, and it was obvious she was angry. Being the wise man that I am, I stayed quiet for a minute before breaking the silence with one of the most absurd things I've ever said: "I told you I knew where the car was."

WRONG TURNS

One summer, my wife and I (David) were driving home from a trip. We were passing through the glorious Appalachian Mountains and were crossing from North Carolina into Tennessee. It was a beautiful June day, and we decided to take a detour through Great Smoky Mountains National Park.

Having been in this part of our home state many times, we thought we remembered a back road leading from the east side of Knoxville up into the Great Smoky Mountains. The conversation went back and forth as we tried to remember how to get where we wanted to go. We weren't coming to any conclusions. Every exit seemed to offer a roundabout route to the Smokies, but with little clarity about where we'd end up. We knew exactly where we wanted to be, just not how to get there. My wife finally *demanded* that we stop wandering and ask for directions.

You have to understand that wandering is something I do well. And I am often reminded of J. R. R. Tolkien's words that "not all who wander are lost." Though Connie appreciates Tolkien's work, she was not willing to embrace his way of thinking on this day, so we argued our way off the interstate at Waynesville. Upon exiting, we discovered that the E-Z Stop Ice Cream Churn was our only option for directions. It didn't look to be a very good option, but sometimes you just have to work with what you've been given. Immediately after stepping out of our Expedition, we realized we were in the middle of Nowheresville. It was reminiscent of the Burt Reynolds movie *Deliverance*.

Connie walked around to the driver's side of the car as I was climbing out. She looked at the empty car parked next to ours and said, "Is that a wig?"

"What?" I looked into the passenger seat and there was a large, long, curly blonde, Dolly Partonish wig resting on the headrest. (I suppose the owner was trying to keep it fresh and ready for wear.) I stared at the faux coiffure for a moment before heading into the E-Z Stop to use the john. I also happened to notice a bumper sticker on the back of the car that read, "Ain't skeered." (I have to admit that the wig and the bumper sticker kinda "skeered" me a bit.)

But that was only a precursor to the parade of characters I would encounter in the next ten minutes. As I entered the store, I noticed that the woman behind the counter (I'm pretty sure it was a woman) had on a Lynyrd Skynyrd muscle tee and her arms were covered with tattoos. She greeted me by saying, "Yeah."

Now, what does that mean? Is that "Welcome to Waynesville, come on in," or does it mean, "I've seen your type before, city boy. You just wanna pee and ask for directions. You ain't gonna buy no gas, are ya?"

Whatever it means, I said it back to her, kinda slow and rough, "Yeah."

She shook her head at me, and I kept walking toward the men's room, which was in the back.

Along the way, I had to walk past some pinball and video

games, where a dad and his daughter were playing pinball. He had a mullet, and she had long straight hair with big puffy bangs. She looked to be about twelve. As I passed by, the man handed the girl a quarter and said, "This is your last one, Tiffany. You ain't gettin' no more after this one, understand me?"

Tiffany was too busy eating Funyuns to respond; but she took the quarter and rolled her eyes. I just kept walking.

I found the men's room. As is often the case, one wall was lined with condom machines, and there were telephone numbers and dirty messages written everywhere. When I was done, I washed my hands twice and tried to open the door with my elbows. Tiffany was still playing her last round, her daddy was shaking his machine, and the bells were ringing. I thanked the lady behind the counter, and she said, "Yeah."

When I stepped outside, I found my wife engaged in a conversation with a couple in the parking lot who would reinforce our sense of being in the middle of nowhere. As I neared the car, I caught a better glimpse.

Well, Connie's found some locals, I'll give her that.

The couple were sitting in a rusty Ford pickup, apparently waiting for something. For what, I don't know. There wasn't room for anyone else to ride with them, and they weren't near the gas pump. I began to wonder if perhaps they were just out for an afternoon drive, enjoying the scenery and a trip to the E-Z Stop.

They looked to be in their early sixties. The woman was wearing big, dark sunglasses, but they weren't *real* sunglasses. They were the kind you get after they dilate your eyes at the optometrist's office. I guess she'd held on to them to get some extra mileage. She had tightly permed hair, the kind all the cafeteria ladies at my elementary school had. Her husband was mostly toothless, with tan, leathery skin. (And he was living proof that you don't need teeth to enjoy Skoal.)

Connie asked for directions, and the man's opening remark was something to the effect of, "Let me start by saying that I don't drive." That seemed strange, considering he was sitting behind the wheel. He went on to say that he "thinks" we should get *back* on the interstate and head down two more exits. "Get off at Pigeon Forge/Sevierville, near them outlet malls, and you'll get to where you're goin'."

I'm thinking, *We're in the middle of nowhere and I'm trusting myself to a man who says he doesn't drive, but who thinks we should head toward the outlet malls.* I glared at my wife on the way back to our vehicle as if to say, "Feel better now, honey?"

That June afternoon, we found our way to where we wanted to go, but in life the outcome isn't always that positive (and the people aren't always that interesting). I more often resist (or refuse) my wife's suggestions about stopping and asking for help. I would rather wander and wander than admit to not knowing where I'm going.

ARE MEN JUST STUPID?

Why are we men like this? How can the stereotype about not asking for directions be so accurate? Why do we have trouble admitting when we're lost?

We need to get a couple of things out on the table concerning this question. First of all, from a male perspective, we're never lost—we just haven't figured out how to get where we want to be . . .

yet. Some part of us is convinced that if we just take that next turn, or drive for a few more minutes, we will somehow end up where we wanted to be in the first place. But life rarely works out that way.

The other thing about men and directions is that we act totally different when we're not with a woman. If two guys were driving somewhere together and they somehow got hopelessly lost, they probably wouldn't hesitate to pull into the next gas station and ask for directions. It's only when there's a woman in the car that we feel compelled to wander in hopes of finding our way.

Of course, this is not some modern-era dilemma that began with the advent of automobiles. We'd venture to guess that even cavemen and cavewomen bickered about which way to go to find the closest mastodons. As the maxim goes, "There is nothing new under the sun," and that's certainly true for how men and women relate to each other. Certainly, men have been slow to ask for directions for a long time.

SPEAK UP, ADAM!

This tension between the sexes has been going on since the beginning of time. In fact, we see hints of it in the very first story told about marriage, that of Adam and Eve in the Garden of Eden. When the serpent came to tempt Eve, Adam's failure to "stop and ask directions"—or to say anything at all—erased innocence from the Garden and brought an end to life in Paradise for Adam and Eve and all their descendants.

Adam's tension wasn't with the serpent. He knew all about serpents (so much so that he had even named them). He may have been thinking something like: *I'm lost, and I don't know what to do. This snake here is telling Eve one thing, and God told me something else. If I speak up, then Eve will see that I really don't know where we are.*

Oh, how it could have been different if Adam had spoken up and admitted to everyone he was lost. Maybe he could have said something like this: "Eve, stop! Let's ask God about this. He comes this way every evening. He will know what to do. I don't know what to do, but he can clear all this up."

But Adam didn't say anything of the sort. He just stood silent, his mouth stuffed with fruit, juices dripping from his chin, and his hands sticky with sin.

It seems that Adam (like most guys) was more concerned with ego preservation than he was with doing what was right. It seems that he might have been more worried about what Eve would think of him than he was with what God had said. It's hard to blame Adam. There was a lot on the line, and just like driving around in the car not knowing how to get where you want to go, it was a no-win proposition—a catch-22. If he stopped and asked for help, Eve would see that he was incompetent. If he kept his mouth shut and Eve found out that he was lost, she would also see that he was incompetent. When he chose to keep silent, his only recourse was to wait and see and hope it all turned out okay on its own. The modern day example of a man and woman driving around lost is simply part of the long shadow cast by the first relational breakdown between Adam and Eve. The same dynamics govern both situations.

WHO'S ASKING ANYWAY?

The question "Why won't men ask for directions?" also says something about women. The question arises partly out of genuine curiosity—"He is different from me, and I don't understand him"—but a closer look reveals that it is actually rooted in a woman's heart and reflects three specific things about her: her anger, her fear, and her disappointment.

Her *anger* arises from a sense of powerlessness. Think about it. Where is the woman when she asks the question? *She's in the passenger seat.* In the healthiest of relationships, this means she's the copilot, but many marriages aren't so healthy.

The question also expresses her *fear* that she is lost and possibly unsafe, and it points to her *disappointment* that she may not get where she wants to go with the one she's with.

If she responds out of her anger, she might say, "Pull over! Let me drive! I will get us there." If she responds out of her fear, she might say, "Do you even know where you are going?" And if she responds out of her disappointment, she might say, "Let's just go home. I'll go by myself." At the core of these three responses is the woman's desire to find a way out of the car and into her own set of wheels. However, in order to choose one of these responses, she must flee from her original design as a partner for the man.

But what is the alternative—to depend on the man? "Why won't men ask for directions?" exposes a woman's internal response to feelings of powerlessness (both her own and the man's). When a man is silent or incompetent or imperfect, it becomes easier for the woman to transfer her sense of powerlessness to him. "It must be his fault!" It's no wonder that Eve ate the fruit and then gave some to Adam. His silence exposed her fear of being alone, unsafe, and powerless.

BEING LOST ISN'T SUCH A BAD THING

Though we may laugh at a man who won't ask for help when he's lost, his reluctance to ask for directions isn't necessarily a negative characteristic. In fact, his persistence in pressing on expresses something good and God given—namely, the hunger for exploration and adventure. John Eldredge captures it well in his book *Wild at Heart:* "Adventure, with all its requisite danger and wildness, is a deeply spiritual longing written into the soul of man."[1] God created men with a desire for exploration, a curiosity for the unseen, and a hunger for adventure. Without adventure and challenge, a man begins to wither.

History books are full of the exploits of brave and curious men who set off toward the horizon in order to quench their thirst for discovery and their longing for a full life. The American spirit uniquely embraces this call to rugged adventure, as seen in the lives of men such as Lewis and Clark, Daniel Boone, Edward H. Harriman, and Neil Armstrong.

Could it be that part of what a man is after, in his reluctance to ask for directions, is a craving for discovery? We say, emphatically, "Yes!" Beneath the pride and powerlessness of a man lost in his car lies something much more pure and noble. The heart of a man is bent toward the wild. We don't have to sail the seas or journey to the moon to experience this quest for adventure; all we have to do is get in the car and drive. The magnificence of a man who is willing to "wing it" is that he can take a woman to places where she would unlikely venture on her own.

THE MORE THINGS CHANGE . . .

David and I (Stephen) recently went to Chicago for some television interviews to promote a book we had written. We arrived at the airport and made our way to the Hertz rental car stand to pick up our ride for the week. Being in such a large city, we opted for a car with a GPS navigation system called Never Lost. This was a piece of technological beauty. No matter where we went in Chicago, we were easily able to find our way to the next location. As we approached a turn, a charming female voice would gently announce, "Right turn ahead in one mile." Even if we missed the turn, she would reconfigure our route and give us new directions. We couldn't get lost if we tried. It occurred to me that if every car were equipped with one of these Never Lost systems, the question of why men won't stop for directions would become irrelevant.

Of course, the whole debate about asking for directions is only a symptom of a deeper, more serious problem—namely, that women really don't trust men, men really don't trust themselves, and neither men nor women really trust God. Consequently, men are often aimless and indecisive, and women are often insecure and resentful. Things haven't changed much since the days of Adam and Eve. Men still want to feel important. Women still want to feel valued. Men want to *do* something that matters. Women want to *be* accepted. Men desire strength and respect. Women desire to be seen and loved. Men want to know where they are going—that their direction is set and their destination is pinpointed. Women want to know who they are—that they are lovely, and that they are safe and grounded and free to be themselves.

This tension between the sexes is full of both dignity and depravity. We all may occasionally get lost along the way, but there's good and bad in everything that transpires between men and women. If we can recognize our own internal experiences and acknowledge them to each other, we may begin to look beyond our differences and recognize our true identity as God's handiwork. As they say, getting there is half the fun.

SO, WHAT'S A WOMAN TO DO?

1. Remember that, at its core, the man's response—"I'm not lost"—speaks to his innate hunger for purpose and adventure.
2. Keep in mind that the question, "Why won't men stop for directions?" also says something about a woman's anger, fear, and disappointment.
3. Don't miss the opportunity that is birthed out of conflict and tension.
4. In response to the other question we raised in this chapter— "Are men just stupid?"—yeah, sometimes we just are.

3
"IN A MINUTE."

IT DIDN'T TAKE much of a conversation for my wife and me (Stephen) to decide that we wanted to add to our family. We already had two wonderful children, and we loved being parents. For us, at that point in our story, it seemed like the next right thing to do. So we began to talk and pray and plan.

Other people in our lives weren't quite so sure it was a good idea. From time to time when the topic of more children came up at family gatherings, they expressed their reservations. Even my mother-in-law, who deeply loves her grandchildren, would ask, "You're done, aren't you?"

Heather and I would answer with something like, "We're not sure. We're thinking we might like more children."

To this, my father-in-law, Joe, would caution us with phrases like, "Two children are plenty," and "Big families are too expensive on today's dollar." At times like this, I would think, *Yeah, Joe, it's not like the good old days when you raised your four kids during the seventies oil crisis, the super-inflation of the eighties, and the recession of the early nineties.* My wife would jokingly reply with something like, "But, I'm *your* third child," or, "Didn't *you* have *four* kids?"

But it wasn't only family members who weighed in on our plans. Total strangers would share their opinions with us. I can remember on more than one occasion someone approaching us at the supermarket or the mall and saying something like, "Oh, what beautiful children you have—a girl and a boy! Well, there's no need for you to have any more kids." The entire time I'm thinking, *Who do you think you are, Planned Parenthood?*

As we began actively trying to add to our family, we realized that if we were going to have more kids, we would need a bigger house. (At that point, we were renting a two-bedroom, two-bath apartment in an older home that was subdivided into thirds.) When spring rolled around, we began house shopping. After several weeks of looking, we found a suitable 1400-square-foot, three-bedroom house. Not too big, but perfect for a soon-to-be (we hoped) family of five. As it turned out, sometime around six weeks after we moved in, Heather became pregnant. Our plan was working out perfectly.

The pregnancy progressed easily. (Well, as easily as it could for a pregnant mother of two children four and under.) As summer came to a close, we announced our pregnancy to family and friends at a Labor Day party (how apropos) at our house. The news was met with surprise and adulation. Every month, we went to the ob-gyn for Heather to get a physical. It being her third pregnancy, these checkups were rather uneventful, and everything progressed without complication.

When the time came in early November for Heather's first sonogram, we were excited and eager to finally see images of our baby. With our previous pregnancies, the ultrasound had been the event where I felt the reality of parenthood begin to settle in. With that in mind, I'd been looking forward to this event for many weeks.

Because we had agreed that this would be our last pregnancy, we decided to bring the kids along to be a part of the experience. I initially had some reservations about having the kids there if there was any chance of bad news coming from the procedure. But after talking it over with Heather, my anxiety was allayed, and I began looking forward to having our four-year-old daughter and barely two-year-old son present. I was excited that we were going to experience this important moment together as a family, and it was a great opportunity for the kids to be introduced to the idea of Mommy having a baby in her tummy. We thought that they would love to see the baby on TV and that it might help them prepare better for the upcoming changes to our family.

It was an early appointment, so we didn't have to wait long before the ultrasound tech, a lanky, middle-aged woman named Mitzy or Itzy or Bitzy—something like that—retrieved us from the lobby and led the way down a winding corridor to the room where she would perform the procedure. Mitzy reminded me of a younger version of my fifth-grade teacher, Mrs. Edwards, who to my adolescent eyes looked nearly eighty years old (though she was probably more like fifty). Mrs. Edwards had an intimidating scowl and a fanatical pickiness about neat cursive handwriting. So, for reasons beyond Mitzy's control, I had an uneasy vibe going into the sonogram room.

The ultrasound equipment was the typical setup, a space-age contraption that looked like something right out of *Star Wars*. Mitzy directed Heather to an adjacent room to put on a gown, while I positioned two chairs beside the bed, one for Emma Claire and one for Elijah. I made small talk for a moment while trying to clear from my head the thought of Mrs. Edwards barking at me about my poor handwriting.

Heather reentered the room in a hospital gown and climbed onto the table. With a little help, the kids scurried onto the chairs so that they could see the monitor, and I positioned myself at the head of the exam table.

The tech squirted the sound-conductive jelly over Heather's belly and smoothed it around using the sonogram apparatus. This worried our daughter a little.

"Daddy, why are they putting glue on Mommy's tummy?" she asked compassionately.

As I tried to explain to my daughter what was going on, I was also wrangling my toddler son. "No, Eli! You *cannot* taste it."

Mitzy turned the monitor toward the head of the bed and moved the sound-wave device across Heather's abdomen. "Is this your first ultrasound with this pregnancy?" she inquired.

Heather glanced at me before saying yes. I intuitively knew that something was not normal.

"Well . . . there are two in there."

Hello?

"Twins?" one of us asked in disbelief.

"Yes. Twins."

Even as the tech spoke, Heather shot me an expression that said, "Stephen, you'd better shut that crazy woman up, because she doesn't know what in the world she's talking about!" But Mitzy of course knew exactly what she was talking about.

As our attention turned to the monitor, we saw our *children* on the screen. "From now on, this will be Baby A, and this one here will be Baby B," the tech said with a whimsical grin. (Was she enjoying this, watching two unsuspecting parents decompensate before her eyes?)

"Baby A and Baby B," I repeated hazily, as I gently put my hand on Heather's forehead. My legs filled with Jell-O, my stomach began somersaulting, and my lips became cold. I was about to faint. Turning toward my daughter, I picked her up and put her in the chair with her brother. "Emma Claire, you gotta move. I have to sit down."

By now, our daughter had caught on. "Two babies!" she exclaimed. "Are there more in there?"

I hope not, I thought as I glanced at the technician.

"No, just two," Mitzy replied.

My daughter descended from the chair and made her way right next to her mother's face. "Emma Claire," Heather said in almost a whisper, "We're having twins—two babies, not just one." This clarification was probably more for herself and me than it was for our daughter.

"Two and two make four," Emma Claire exclaimed.

"Yes, honey, two and two do make four," Heather confirmed. We were no longer doing addition—we were now into multiplication.

I excused myself, stepped out into the hall, and called my

brother-in-law to come get the kids. Heather and I were going to need to be alone for a while to make sense of all this. When I reentered the exam room, Heather was trembling like she had chills.

"Are you cold?" I asked.

"No, I just can't stop shaking." She was in shock. We both were.

The tech proceeded with the exam. Beginning with Baby A, she measured all its parts: femur, stomach, kidneys, head, face, and brain—evaluating everything twice. Then she switched to Baby B and ran through the same procedure. It took almost an hour to complete the exam. Toward the end, the tech asked, "Do you want to find out the sex?"

I looked at Heather enthusiastically.

"What do *you* think?" Heather asked.

"You know what I think. I want to know," I responded. "But it's up to you. If you want to wait, I'll wait."

"I guess I want to know," she said. (Back when we thought we were having only one baby, Heather had half-capitulated one evening when I was pressuring her to find out the baby's sex at the ultrasound: "The only way I want to know the sex is if we're having twins." At the time, neither one of us thought that was a possibility.)

"Boys," the tech declared.

We were expecting twin boys in the spring. What are the odds? I soon found out that the natural occurrence of twins not tied to fertility drugs is one out of eighty-nine births.[1] (With numbers like that, I should have left the doctor's office, hopped in the car, and raced to buy a lottery ticket.)

Naturally, we were overjoyed and overwhelmed. I remember thinking as we drove home, *I guess God knows what he's doing—I just wish I knew what he's doing.* As we eased up to a stop sign, I said something to Heather like, "I could've dreamed up any number of things that could've happened today at the doctor's office (good and bad), but this—this just came out of nowhere." When will I ever learn that I can't outdream God?

Fast-forward now several more months to early March. We went in one day late in the pregnancy for a regular checkup. A few minutes into the exam, the doctor said (far too casually, if you ask me), "Well, it looks like we're going to have some babies today." A few hours—and several thousand dollars—later, Heather and I were the proud parents of two awesome boys, Henry and Teddy.

Transitioning to our new life was hard. It took a few months to get our hearts and heads around it all. To get a picture of what it looked like, you need to understand three things: 1) little sleep, 2) very little sleep, and 3) very, very little sleep. There were times in the first several months when Heather and I were both so tired that some strange things happened—such as finding our house keys in the refrigerator, driving the wrong baby to the pediatrician, falling asleep while eating dinner, wearing two different shoes to the grocery store. . . Things like that.

EXIT STAGE LEFT

One day, a few months into our new life as a family of six, I came home from work and walked into utter chaos: babies crying, phone ringing, older kids squabbling, dog barking at her food bowl, tired wife needing assistance. Gone was the *Father Knows Best* fantasy of calling out, "Honey, I'm home," and being greeted with the day's newspaper, a sampling of hors d'oeuvres, and a cocktail so

Pops could unwind. No, this was all hands on deck! Iceberg off the port bow! Man the lifeboats! The ship is going down!

After several moments of helping out as best I could, the bedlam had not eased, but my anxiety level had risen. I looked to escape.

"Does the dog need to go out?" I asked.

"No, I took her out earlier," Heather said.

"Do you need anything from the store?" I tried again.

"That's okay. My mother came by today and brought us some things. Thanks though."

"Well, I'm going to excuse myself and go to the bathroom," I said.

"Okay, but we need to get the older kids dinner and a bath," Heather gently reminded me.

I went into the bathroom, locked the door, and parked myself on the edge of the tub. I stared at the floor for several moments, just sitting there.

The babies were still crying, and I could hear my poor, overloaded wife calling from the other room, "Stephen, I need your help."

"In a minute," I replied. "I'm still in the bathroom."

"Honey, are you sick? Do you need anything?" my sweet wife asked.

"No, I'm fine. I'll be out in a minute."

A few more minutes passed before my daughter knocked on the door. "Daddy, when are you going to be out? Mommy said she needs help feeding the babies."

"Tell Mommy I'm almost done. I'll be out in a minute." Oh great, now I was lying to my innocent daughter. I pulled myself together, flushed the toilet and washed my hands for good measure, unlocked the door, and left my inner sanctum.

As I came out of the bathroom, my wife remarked to me, "Why do men spend so much time on the toilet?"

"I dunno."

Am I a coward? Some would say so. I'd rather have people just assume I have an active colon. (Though I'm not sure why that's any better.) How does that saying go? When the going gets tough . . . the tough get out of Dodge.

HITTING THE MARK

The male instinct to hide is well played out in a great film by John Hughes titled *She's Having a Baby*. The movie chronicles the life of a young couple, from their wedding day through the birth of their first child. The story of Jake and Kristy Briggs (played by Kevin Bacon and Elizabeth McGovern) is both hilarious and poignant. It's a valid picture of a man's fear and insecurity.

Midway through the story, we pick up with Jake and Kristy in the midst of a long journey of trying to get pregnant. Kristy has been in for a checkup and informs Jake that her doctor confirmed that there's absolutely nothing wrong with her body that would prevent her from getting pregnant. From this news, she deduces that Jake is obviously the one responsible for their infertility. She coerces him into taking a sperm sample in for observation. The test reveals that Jake's body temperature is contributing to a low sperm count, all dictated by his preference in underwear.

In a pivotal scene, we find Jake down in the basement, pretending to be working on the hot water heater. Instead, he's actually throwing darts—throwing darts and hiding—hiding from the news, hiding from his wife, hiding from the idea of becoming a dad, hiding from himself. Every once in a while, he picks up a tool and bangs it against the hot water heater to create the illusion of purpose and productivity.

Meanwhile, Kristy is upstairs in the bedroom. She is taking her temperature, charting her menstrual cycle, and attempting to master the science of conception. We see her sitting amidst a bed of pillows arranged according to the fertility doc's recommendation to maximize conception opportunities. All around her are charts, thermometers, and other instruments. She begins calling out for Jake as she realizes her body temperature is optimal.

Kristy: "Jake. Jakey. My temperature's just right. This is the perfect time. Where are you?"

Down in the basement, Jake turns toward the stairs to acknowledge her plea and then turns back to the darts, pretending not to hear her. Kristy calls out to him repeatedly as he continues to stare ahead and throw darts.

Kristy: "Can you hurry?"

He bangs on the water heater.

Kristy: "Jakey, my temperature's just right. Where are you? Hurry, hurry!"

He sits paralyzed, staring ahead.

Kristy (at the top of her lungs): "Jefferson Edward Briggs!"

Jake emerges from the basement with a look of utter despair, his face plagued with fear and shame. Kristy regains her composure and greets him.

Kristy: "Hi, babe. Were you working on the water heater again?"

He nods sheepishly, like a boy trying to convince his mother that he *did* indeed clean his room.

Kristy: "I'm sorry to interrupt you, but it's been forty-eight hours since our last coition. My temperature is optimum. I'm ovulating. I have the pillows set up in the position Dr. Stanky wants us to try so that my cervix is placed better in the intervaginal seminal pool."

Jake sighs deeply with the same look of fear and despair plastered across his face. Kristy doesn't react. Instead, she reaches over to grab glasses of champagne for the two of them and continues talking with great determination.

Kristy: You can watch TV if you get bored."

She raises her glass to offer a toast.

Kristy: "Here's to successful fertilization, sweetie."

She immediately goes back to reading her charts. Jake downs the entire glass of champagne, reacts to the bitter taste of it all, and then slowly drops his pants to the floor, revealing baggy, oversized boxers. The sound track turns to the old Sam Cooke song, "That's the sound of the men working on the chain gang."

HIDE 'N' GO SEEK

Our old friend Adam, from the book of Genesis, wasn't much different from Jake Briggs. Remember that little mistake with Eve and the serpent and the fruit—the moment where it all went south? When the shame hit the fan and things got complicated, Adam did the only reasonable thing he could do: He ran for cover. He grabbed Eve and made for the trees (because, as far as we know, he didn't yet have a bathroom or a basement to hide in).

Since the beginning of time, men have been hiding in one spot or another—running from their shame and anxiety. The really sad part is that, when a man hides, the woman in his life pays the price. Unless a man overcomes his fear through faith, courage, and freedom, it inevitably leads to control, manipulation, and bondage.

When God came walking in the Garden as the sun was setting, the heat of the day had eased, and a cool evening breeze began to blow, his heart was full of sorrow. He moved through the Garden, looking for Adam and Eve, having just witnessed their betrayal. Beauty had been marred, and there would have to be consequences. With three simple words, God brought the Garden narrative to a climax, as he called out to Adam, "Where are you?"

Adam hollered from somewhere in the bushes, "I heard you in the garden, and I was afraid because I was naked; so I hid."

And then God asked other questions, "Who told you that you were naked? Have you eaten from the tree that I commanded you not to eat from?"

Adam answered, "The woman you put here with me—she gave me some fruit from the tree, and I ate it."

Then God said to Eve, "What is this you have done?"

Eve responded, "The serpent deceived me, and I ate."[2]

It's really quite a ridiculous dialogue.

God asked plainly, "Where, what, who, how?"

Adam, ever so brave, blamed God and Eve. It was as if he said, "Come on, God. I mean, it was your idea to make the woman. Remember? I was taking a nap, and the next thing I knew there's this woman here. What's a guy to do? Anyhow, I was minding my own business when Eve here started yakking it up with a talking snake. Then she gave me some fruit from the tree, and I ate it."

Eve, not to have the debacle pinned on her, rebutted, "Don't look at me, God. It was the snake. He tricked me."

God asked simple and direct questions. Adam and Eve gave multipart and indirect answers. Even though they were busted, they were still trying to hide. In the counseling profession, we refer to this as "blame shifting" or "not taking ownership." Call it what you will, but it's just another form of hiding—hiding the truth. Adam hid himself, he hid his wife, he hid the truth, and he hid his role in the whole exchange.

COME OUT! COME OUT! WHEREVER YOU ARE!

This scene in the Garden with Adam is only one of many accounts in the Bible of people trying to run and hide from God. Beginning with Adam, some of the more familiar hiders include Cain, Moses, David, Jonah, Elijah, and Peter.

Why do men tend to hide? Two reasons: 1) We hope not to be found, and 2) we hope not to be found out. We're crying out, "Please don't expose me for who I really am, and for how really incompetent I am."

I (David) mentioned earlier that I work primarily with

children and adolescents, and I am continually amazed at how kids admit to wanting to be caught by their parents. There's a certain sense of safety that comes with being exposed. The deal's off at that point. There's no more hiding, and the only fear remaining is what the consequence will be. Though they would never tell this to their parents, I've heard dozens of adolescents confess to being relieved when their parents caught them drinking and grounded them. The reason? It took the pressure off to say to their peers, "I'm grounded, and I can't go out tonight." They don't have to battle peer pressure that encourages them to do something illegal.

The secret desire to be found comes in many forms. For example, another boy told me years ago that when he felt lonely, he would ride his bike in a heavily populated area of his neighborhood, purposely fall off his bike, and wait until someone stopped to check on him. This same kid confessed that at camp he would wander down to the dock and stand looking at the water, waiting for someone to come down and ask why he was hanging out alone. Sometimes we all just want to be found. It's like the classic game of hide and seek. There's a thrill that comes from finding an extraordinary place to hide that no one can find, but also the thrill of being discovered. As men, we feel an intense fear about being found out, but there is also a sense of relief and safety when we come out of hiding.

I can remember multiple occasions of running away from home. I grew up in a really small town, and you could only go so far without bumping into someone who knew you or your family. The Yateses would be out in their front yard and would look up and say, "There goes David, running away again."

My parents lost count of how many times I threatened to

leave home or actually packed my bags. In fact, they eventually got to the point where they would offer to help me pack my things. My mom would ask, "Do you want a suitcase from the basement or just your backpack this time?"

They have memories of me at nine years old launching out the back door and reminding my family members of how sad they would all be when I was gone. "I'm for real this time, and you'll all be really sad you lost such a great son!" (I could get theatrical with the best of them.)

It wasn't until I was in my thirties that my mom told me that she and my dad would go upstairs and watch me out of the bedroom window as I kicked trees, mouthed off, and headed for the street behind our house, dragging my belongings and stuffed Snoopy.

I would turn around periodically to see if anyone was coming after me, begging me to stay, but they were all perched upstairs by this time for a balcony view of the drama. They must have ducked down below the windowsill every time I turned around, to make certain I didn't see them watching and laughing hysterically from the second story of our old house.

Usually, I'd go to the end of the street and camp out under some neighbor's tree, wait about half an hour, and then go home. Once, I stayed for an hour, but I always got hungry and went home. And I always wanted to be found and welcomed home.

OLLIE OLLIE OXEN FREE

Isn't it curious that God's first utterance to Adam and Eve after it all went bad in the Garden was not some grand theological statement? Nor was it a doctrinal clarification of Adam and Eve's misunderstanding of the rule to not eat the fruit. This is the same God who created all existence from nothingness by simply speaking; so he certainly knew *where* Adam and Eve were hiding, and he certainly knew *why* they were hiding. So what's with all the questions?

God's question is an *invitation* to Adam, not an accusation or indictment. God's question is a chance for Adam to do what he failed to do earlier in the story: ask for help and be present in the moment. Adam couldn't hide from God, and neither can we. But that doesn't keep any of us from trying, does it?

Nothing can stay hidden forever. Paul's first letter to his protégé Timothy reminds us of this: "The sins of some men are obvious, reaching the place of judgment ahead of them; the sins of others trail behind them. In the same way, good deeds are obvious, and even those that are not cannot be hidden."[3]

In Galatians, Paul says it a little more forcefully: "Do not be deceived: God cannot be mocked. People reap what they sow."[4] It's kind of like the old saying: "It all comes out in the wash."

Adam and Eve resisted coming out. They refused to tell God the truth. Men and women have been hiding ever since. But it's not until we come out of hiding that we will come to know the love that we were created to experience. It's the meaning of the line from the old hymn, "I once was lost, but now am found." God calls to each of us, "Come out, come out, wherever you are." His intent is not to punish us, but instead to set us free—free to be with him and to enjoy each other.

SO, WHAT'S A WOMAN TO DO?

1. Remember that no matter what kind of front a man puts up, he is afraid of being revealed as incompetent. This will

explain a great deal of what you experience when a man is put on the spot.

2. It is always better to *invite* a man to conversation rather than forcing him into it.

3. If you hear a man clanging around in the basement, you know he's scared to death of something.

"CAN'T IT WAIT TILL HALFTIME?"

WHAT'S THE DEAL WITH GUYS AND SPORTS?

I (STEPHEN) HAVE A FRIEND, Sarah, who recently started dating a guy. Their relationship is in its early stages, and Sarah is high on the exhaust fumes of romance. You've probably been there. You can't eat, you can't sleep, and your heart jumps with hope whenever the phone rings. The early indications are that this could be Sarah's Mr. Right, and she's distracted by what this relationship could become.

As she and I have talked about this guy, I've likened where she is to the anticipation one feels on a roller coaster: Having just left the terminal, they are slowly inching their way up the steep incline that will launch them on the ride. You can almost hear the *click, click, click, click, click* in the background when she talks about this man.

The guy Sarah's been seeing is a high school coach. This has not been an obstacle for their relationship, because Sarah likes sports and has participated in sports in the past. (While growing up, she was a nationally ranked competitive athlete.) Lately, she's been going to Coach's games to cheer him on. After the games, they usually grab a bite to eat and hang out the rest of the evening. One evening following a game, she and Coach went for a picnic, but he was generally depressed and preoccupied much of the time. Sarah went home confused, wondering if she had misread the relationship. Was this budding romance coming to an end before it ever really began?

The next day, Sarah and I were talking about her evening with Coach, and she was expressing her disappointment. She was bemoaning how it had turned out and questioning what went wrong. As she told the story, I wondered aloud, "Did his team win or lose?"

"They lost. Why?"

"Sarah, he was in a bad mood because he lost, not because of being with you. Men don't like to lose."

She paused to think it over. "Well, he did say that was the reason. I just couldn't believe that it could really be losing that would matter so much."

"Oh, believe me. It matters," I said. "Please tell me you didn't say, 'It doesn't matter that you lost.'"

"No, I'm not that stupid," Sarah said, "but what's the deal with guys and sports?"

Great question! What *is* the deal with guys and sports?

PLAY BALL

The preschool my (David's) daughter attended hosted a Father's Day event every year. The dads would show up for a hot dog and lemonade lunch and games in the gymnasium. The school had a carnival set up where dads could engage in activities with their little ones. My daughter and I rotated from the bean bag toss and water gun extravaganza to a station where she gave me a mock shave with real shaving cream (but no blade in the razor, thank God).

The day's events culminated with the annual tug-of-war contest, in which the dads from the Pre-K One class took on the dads from the Pre-K Two class. You can just imagine the spectacle—a bunch of middle-aged men, on two sides of the gym, dressed in starched shirts and neckties, testosterone raging as they yanked on the rope, reliving their elementary school days. During my daughter's last year of preschool, the Pre-K Two dads lost the tug-of-war, and I am still recovering from it. It nearly killed me (pulling a rope that hard *and* the taste of defeat).

What's that all about? That force of nature that rises up in us as men where we get so outrageously competitive. We can't stop, we can't let up, and we can't give in. Sometimes we're not even aware it's still in us. Then it shows up, and we're like twelve-year-old boys at a track meet all over again, and the gun is about to fire.

RUNNERS, ON YOUR MARKS!

Adam and Eve were no strangers to what happens when competition between men runs amok. They witnessed it firsthand with their children Cain and Abel.[1] The story goes that Cain, a farmer, and Abel, a herder, both brought offerings to God. Cain brought some grain, and Abel brought some fat from an animal in his herd. Though Cain was the first to think of this and bring his offering to God, God liked Abel's offering better. This really ticked off Cain, and he walked away angry and depressed.

God, being who he is, asked Cain a couple of questions: "Why are you angry? Why is your face downcast? If you do what is right, will you not be accepted? But if you do not do what is right, sin is crouching at the door; it desires to have you, but you must rule over it."

This made Cain all the more angry. First, his offering got second place, and then God made a point of wanting to talk about it all. Why couldn't God just let it rest? In his rage, Cain tricked his brother, Abel, to come with him out in a field. Once Cain had Abel on his own turf (home field advantage), Cain killed him and hid the body. But God, ever persistent, showed up to ask an obvious question, much as he had with Adam and Eve: "Where's your brother Abel?"

To which Cain replied with something to the effect of, "I don't know. Who do you think I am, his babysitter?" Talk about a sore loser.

This sense of competition still runs in our blood today. A recent Google search on "fantasy baseball" resulted in 48,000,000 hits. That's 48 *m-i-l-l-i-o-n!* If you aren't familiar with fantasy sports leagues, they are kind of a combination of Dungeons and Dragons and baseball trading cards for adults. ESPN.com, a hub for many fantasy league enthusiasts, has leagues for every major sport: baseball, football, basketball, hockey, and soccer, as well as for many other activities like stock car racing, bass fishing (yes, fishing), poker, and horse racing.

Although the rules and structure vary from league to league, a typical league involves a group of guys getting together (either in person or online) prior to a specific sport's season and pretending to be owners, general managers, and coaches of professional sports franchises. They "draft" players onto their teams and then use the players' real-life statistics to determine the outcome of fantasy games throughout the season. Over the course of the season, players can improve their teams through "unlimited trades" and "free agent signings," in hopes of making it all the way to the "championship."

Sports fantasy leagues give us a glimpse of what men are looking for from sports. Sports are a way for men to express themselves without the fear of serious consequences or failure. They're a way for men to go to war without having to die. Fantasy leagues are an even safer extension of sports competition—a way to compete without having to pull a muscle or even get off the couch. The most dangerous thing that can happen in a fantasy league is carpal tunnel syndrome, or maybe tendinitis in an index finger, from clicking the computer mouse too much.

THE LOVE DOCTOR

Nashville is an easy place to spot celebrities. Many a famous person calls Nashville home. And I (David) am not just talking about country music stars. The city is full of celebrities. A friend of mine just had breakfast at a table next to Nicole Kidman at Bread and Company. I saw John Corbett (that guy from *Northern Exposure* and *Sex and the City*) last week. Sheryl Crow, Steve McNair, Nikki Taylor, Ashley Judd—and her Italian race-car driving husband—all have homes in Nashville. And why not? It's an incredible place to live—great art, excellent food, major sports teams, all sorts of historical sites (Studio B, where Elvis cut many of his records, and

Andrew Jackson's home, the Hermitage, just to name two), great climate with all four seasons, and on and on. The city is not too big, but just big enough. A perfect place to live, in my opinion.

I work out at a local YMCA, where I'll occasionally encounter a celebrity or two. I recently had one of my ultimate celebrity encounters. I found myself exercising next to the incomparable Emmylou Harris (whom I have an enormous crush on).

So, there I was, sweating on the elliptical machine with my iPod, listening to *Wrecking Ball*, one of her older recordings, when she got on the machine next to mine. My heart started racing, I couldn't breathe very well, and I drew a complete blank on how to move my arms and legs simultaneously. I thought to myself, *What if I was singing out loud or humming (which I've been known to do from time to time) when she approached? Oh, God, what an idiot I am! What if she is next door thinking, "Great, I'm trying to get a little cardio in, and I land next to some freaky stalker"?*

The dialogue continued in my head, and I began developing a safety plan.

Okay, here's your strategy. You're going to get off the machine and move to another location. You're not capable of being this close to Emmylou Harris. Don't even think about having a conversation with her, you Goober. Stay silent, look straight ahead, act cool, and get off the machine.

I slowed down the intensity to the single digits and calmly stepped off—first with one foot and then the other.

You're doing well, buddy, just take it slow and don't look her in the eye—'cause if you do, you might ask her to autograph your forehead.

As I turned to step away quickly from the machine, I felt a

pull on my back foot. My lace had gotten caught in the step. But it was too late—I had already stepped forward with my front foot.

I began to fall forward, with the full force of my body weight, into the handlebars of the elliptical machine, entangling myself in the pedals, the mount, and the electrical cord. It was *humiliating!* I wanted the floor to swallow me whole. I managed to draw attention from almost every person on the lower level of the wellness area.

I instantly thought of the time a friend of mine fell while modeling in front of more than a thousand people. She recalled the moment of humiliation as she tumbled down a small flight of stairs in stilettos and a tight, long dress. The audience rose and gasped as she bounded toward the ground. She said that when she landed, she did the only thing she knew to do in the face of that kind of humiliation. She immediately leapt to her feet, in her heels and gown, and threw her hands high in the air, as an Olympic gymnast would following a stellar performance on the balance beam. The crowd started screaming and applauding her.

I wanted so badly to do something that courageous. I wanted to recover with a flourish that would have me bowing on one knee and professing my love. *I love you, Emmylou. I love your music. I love your voice. I love the way you play the guitar and tell those deep, tragic stories in your lyrics. When you sing "Wayfaring Stranger" or "Red Dirt Girl," I am mesmerized. I've loved you for years, and I can't believe we're here together at the Y, doing cardio side by side.*

And then it occurred to me. *David, you are a grown man. You have a wife and three children. You are a professional. And you are floundering around on the floor, tangled up in the cardio*

51

equipment, blubbering over a country-music singer who is fifty-something years old (but drop-dead gorgeous at fifty, I might add). Get up off the floor, and control yourself! There is absolutely no excuse for this.

I untangled myself, stood up, and started laughing a ridiculous laugh (like I meant to fall and make a complete fool of myself). No one around me was laughing, though; they were looking at me with pity. A woman passed by and said, "Are you hurt at all? I saw you fall from the other side of the room."

There was simply no way to recover from this spectacle, so I grabbed my iPod, thanked her for her concern, and headed for the locker room. The next day, I had an enormous bruise on my left arm (that I secretly referred to in my mind as "Pancho" on my "Lefty"—you know, from the Emmylou Harris song "Pancho & Lefty"), and I thought about Emmylou on and off throughout the afternoon.

Two days later, I returned to the Y and had *another* star encounter. This time I was riding a stationary bike, reading a *People* magazine from the rack next to me, when this guy mounted the bike on my right. It was Dr. Travis Stork, better known as *The Bachelor: Paris*. This guy has been in every newspaper, on all three networks in Nashville, and the talk of every morning radio show in the city. You see, he's a doctor from Nashville. And the gal he chose from his dating extravaganza in Paris was a school teacher, also from Music City. With reality shows being all the rage, can you just imagine how many Travis and Sarah "sightings" there have been in Nashville?

Well, I was reading the local paper one day when it mentioned how Travis had been sighted several times at a local YMCA and at restaurants throughout the city. I thought to myself, *Poor guy, he can't even lift weights and get a burger without someone tracking his every movement.*

So here I am, cycling at the Y, and Dr. Travis jumps on next to me. Because I'm not fascinated with Travis and Sarah (the way I am with Emmylou), I stayed put and continued pedaling. I had never watched an episode of *The Bachelor* (nor had any interest, for that matter), but I did somehow see the last thirty minutes of the first episode of the Paris season, with the two Nashvillians. (I think it may have been one night while I was exercising, and it was on the screen in front of me.)

Did you see that episode? It was the one where one of the contestants, who was also a doctor, told Travis that she knew the two of them had sacrificed much of their lives to the pursuit of their careers, and she was ready to get down to business and procreate. How's that for an introduction? "Hey, it's great to meet you. How interesting that we're both doctors. What a lovely city Paris is. Let's skip the small talk—wanna make babies together?"

This introduction seemed to freak the Bachelor out a bit (as it would almost every man I know), and so he sent her home on the first night.

Well, it got better. The woman left somewhat teary and exited the castle where the show was being filmed. But when she got out in the driveway, Dr. Jekyll turned into Ms. Hyde. She spun around and came back inside to find the good doctor. When she found him, she whipped the poor guy around and worked him over pretty good. She went nuts! She laid him out about being rejected and wanted to know why. I thought about bringing up the incident with Travis, just to make sure he had recovered. But then I remembered at the end of the show there was a preview for the next week and he was in a hot tub, drinking champagne with, like, ten women, and he looked like he was doing just fine. So, I let it go and continued cycling.

As I pedaled, I had a good time watching women all around us watching Dr. Travis's every move while pretending not to notice him at all. Some of the women were openly staring. Every once in a while, one would approach him to have a conversation and flirt for a few moments. Some of them were trying to "accidentally" bump into him. Most of them looked ridiculous (much the way I must have looked in my encounter with Emmylou).

One woman was talking with her girlfriend, and I could tell that she had positioned her girlfriend's head so that she could stare over her shoulder at the Bachelor while pretending to listen to what her friend was saying. I was fascinated by the attention being given to this man (and I've never had so many women looking in my direction).

As I continued to exercise next to Dr. Travis, I turned the page of my *People* magazine—and lo and behold, there he was, in Paris with Sarah. *This is hysterical,* I thought. I turned the magazine slightly away so he couldn't see that I was reading about him. As I read, I was struck by the similarities between the two of us.

One, we're both from Nashville.

Two, we're both guys.

Three, we're both in a helping profession. He's a doctor, and I'm a therapist.

Four, he works at the Vanderbilt University Medical Center emergency room. I once went to the Vandy ER when I slammed my forehead into a stairwell and had to have eight stitches between my eyes.

Five, according to the article, he likes to play basketball. I was a point guard for Burger Chef when I was in fifth grade.

Six, we're both in our thirties. He's in the early part of the thirties, and I'm closer to the end (but it's the same decade).

Seven, he spent time in Paris, living in a castle with dozens of beautiful women. I once traveled to Europe and stayed in a youth hostel *near* a castle, and there were a lot of girls staying there that night.

Eight, he's very tall—and built. I'm kinda tall (well, I'm not quite six feet, but I'm like five-eleven-and-a-half, which is just shy of six feet) and I'm also built (though built kinda like the Pillsbury Doughboy, soft and squishy all over, like you wanna push on my tummy and make me giggle).

Nine, he seems to always be surrounded by women. I spent eighteen years of my life surrounded by women. My mom is a woman, and so is my sister. We had a dog named Suzy, and we once had two cats, both of whom were female.

It's stunning how much I have in common with this guy.

Just as I was thinking of all the similarities between me and Travis Stork, a very attractive woman approached—approached *me*. She was smiling, and as she sauntered toward me and put her hands on the handlebars of my bike somewhat seductively, I pulled the headphones out of my ears to acknowledge her.

"Hi," she began. "I was wondering when you were planning to be finished on this bike?"

I looked at Dr. Travis. He smiled sheepishly and looked down with an expression that seemed to say, "I'm sorry. I can't control this stuff."

I handed over my station to the desperate young lady and headed over to do some sit-ups.

I was on sit-up number fifty-eight when I noticed someone doing sit-ups next to me. I glanced out of the corner of my eye and saw it was Dr. Travis again. He must've wanted to escape his cycling companion, Female Stalker #226. So, there we were, doing our sit-ups. *Seventy-three, seventy-four, seventy-five. Come on, David, just try to get to one hundred.* As I wrapped it up, I noticed that Dr. Travis was continuing. He even switched around to do some crunches with his legs elevated, using a medicine ball, and then doing some side crunches with weights in each hand.

Well, I wasn't about to let the Bachelor outdo me. *The Love Doctor is not going to show me up,* I said to myself. So, I kicked it up a notch. I put *my* feet up in the air, I bent my knees, I straightened my legs, I did sit-ups with a medicine ball, and I flipped over and did that thing with your body where you bend your arms at the elbow and just hold your body straight. (I don't know how that really works your abs, but I saw Dr. Travis do it and it seemed to be working for him.) I just kept doing more and more. He kept going and so did I.

The next day, I could barely move. *These celebrity sightings are killing me!* I couldn't move my torso because my stomach was in a knot from all those sit-ups. It hurt to sit, it hurt to stand, it hurt when I reached in my closet to get a shirt for work, it hurt when I bent down to pick up my computer bag, and it even hurt to turn the steering wheel in the car. When my son ran to greet me that morning and jumped up on my back, I teared up and silently screamed in agony because it hurt so bad. And, remember, my arm still hurt from Pancho on my Lefty. I was walking and moving like a postsurgical patient. And I felt *so-o-o* ridiculous.

FANATICS

If you are one of those people who believes that men can't communicate their feelings as well as women can, all you have to do is listen to any sports radio call-in show between 4:00 PM and 7:00 PM to hear men pour out their heartache, angst, and hope for their favorite teams. If this were a show about dating, would most of the callers be men? Heck no. But start talking about sports, and the men come out of the woodwork.

As you may know, the term *sports fan* is short for "sports fanatic." *Fanatic* is a word that is normally reserved for folks who have extreme and sometimes irrational enthusiasms or beliefs, especially about religion or politics—but also about sports. Sports fans typically get more upset than the players about wins and losses. Psychologists say that the emotions (and the sex drive) of men who are serious sports fans rise and fall with their teams' performances, because these guys so closely identify with their teams.

Andrew called to make an appointment with me (Stephen) for counseling. It was around the second week of April a few years ago. When we met in my office, a few days later, for an initial interview, Andrew warned me, "Just so you know, I think all this counseling stuff is pretty much crap."

Nothing like having a client's confidence.

As I continued the interview, Andrew let me know that his anger and anxiety had gotten so bad over the past several weeks that his fiancée had demanded he go see a counselor.

In giving me an overview of his life, Andrew mentioned that he worked as a computer systems administrator at an accounting firm. I deduced—rather brilliantly, I thought—that it must be the job stress of the tax season that was getting to him. So I interjected, "I bet that work can get really stressful this time of year, with tax season and all." (I amaze myself sometimes at how intuitive I am.)

Andrew just stared at me. He nodded in agreement, but his face was marked with confusion. "I guess so."

Poor guy, I mused, *He's more disconnected than he realizes.* "Why don't you tell me a little more about your job," I said. *He's lucky to be seeing me. I can really help him.* I gave myself a mental high five.

"Work's really not too bad," Andrew said. "The entire firm is busy with tax prep right now, so they pretty much leave me alone."

Oh, he must be in denial. "How long have you been stressed at work?"

"Work is okay. I generally like what I do," Andrew said, sticking to his story.

"Well, if it's not work, what is it?" *I'll just work with his resistance. Sooner or later, he'll come back around.*

"You'll laugh," he said. "It's kind of embarrassing."

Aha. If it's not work, it probably has something to do with sex. "I promise you, there isn't much I haven't heard."

"You're sure?"

"I can't help you if you don't let me." *Yep, it's got to do with sex.*

"Well, I pushed this guy at work the other day."

"Go on." *Now we are getting somewhere; I knew it had to do with work.*

"Do you watch basketball? Did you see any of the NCAA Tournament?" (It was April and "March Madness," the NCAA national basketball tournament had just ended.)

"I saw some of the games," I said. "Why?"

"Did you see the final?"

"Yes, the second half." *Where is this going?*

"So you know that Georgia Tech lost."

"Yeah, to Connecticut, right? How is that connected to what happened at work?"

"Georgia Tech. That's how." Andrew said, growing agitated.

"Can you tell me what happened?"

"I went nuts. I kicked my TV. I screamed at my fiancée. The next day at work, I freaked out on this guy who was giving me a hard time about UConn winning. I cussed at him, pushed him, and slammed the door to my office. It was really bad. My boss threatened to put me on probation."

"Georgia Tech lost?" I didn't know what else to say, so I just repeated myself, "Tech lost . . . Tech lost," as empathetically as possible. Finally, I asked, "So you're a sports fan?"

"Yeah. I guess you could say that."

"What are your teams?"

"The Braves and the Falcons. I'm from Atlanta, so I follow the Hawks a little; but generally it's the Braves and the Falcons." (I followed sports enough to know that he was talking about baseball, football, and basketball, and not some kind of tribal warfare.)

"And Georgia Tech," I inserted.

"That's where I went to school. I played ball there."

"Oh yeah? What did you play?" I asked.

"Baseball. Did you play sports?"

This is where I had to confess one of my darkest manhood athletic secrets. "Yeah. I played sports in college. I played soccer." (To most male sports fans—especially 6-foot-3-inch, 185 lb. jocks like Andrew—soccer is "a communist sport.")

"Oh, my brother's daughter plays soccer," Andrew said, and I knew he was probably thinking, *No wonder you're a counselor. You played a sissy sport.*

"Why don't you tell me more about the altercation you had in your office," I said.

PUT UP YOUR DUKES

One of the most insightful movies about men in recent years is *Fight Club,* starring Edward Norton and Brad Pitt. It's a disturbing and violent movie that's hard to shake. The movie is narrated by Edward Norton's character, Jack, a mild-mannered automobile manufacturer employee who suffers from insomnia. Jack has been numbed by the day-in-and-day-out grind of his monotonous white-collar job. He has grown materialistic and lacks anything in his life to make him feel alive.

Depressed, Jack visits his doctor for help. The doctor tells him to stop whining and suggests that Jack meet some people who really have problems—like some men who have survived testicular cancer. So Jack visits a support group full of these guys. He soon grows addicted to attending the support group meetings and starts visiting a different group each night of the week. He finds life by pretending to have real problems.

On an airplane one day, he meets Tyler (played by Brad Pitt). They develop a relationship that culminates in a fistfight with each other—and they find it brings them more alive than they have ever been. As other men find out about this unique form of self-help therapy, the "Fight Club" is created, an underground group that encourages men to beat each other up in order to reclaim their manhood by getting in touch with their primal instincts.

There is a lot not to like about this film: abject violence, vandalism, rebellion, chaos, murder, a view of humanity as basically animalistic and hedonistic. But there is also a lot *to* like. Without spoiling the outcome of the movie for you if you haven't seen it, its point is clear: Men are most alive when they feed their needs for adventure, freedom, and passion.

So, what's up with guys and sports? It has to do with feeling good about ourselves without having to do anything—not even get off the couch. It's about experiencing our design without having to risk the consequences.

Have you ever watched kids on the swings? Boys and girls swing in very different ways. The other day, I (Stephen) was swinging my two oldest children in our backyard. My six-year-old daughter wanted to swing to the clouds. "Daddy, push me higher and higher." She kept wanting me to push her and her brother so that they would swing in perfect synchronization. "We are swinging together!" she would exclaim with exhilaration.

My three-year-old son was a bit different. His imagination was running wild. He was Tarzan . . . and Superman . . . and Spiderman . . . and Buzz Lightyear, all at the same time. His heart was on fire for adventure. With a boy's wide-open heart, anything is possible. God is real. Doubt does not exist. You see, for boys, imagination and faith aren't that different. Little boys are bold to believe in something.

Some people call that immature or childish. But it's actually close to how we were made to live. Jesus told people to be like this. In the Gospel of Matthew Jesus called a child over to stand with him. "I tell you the truth," Jesus said, "unless you change and become like little children, you will never enter the kingdom of heaven. Therefore, whoever humbles himself like this child is the greatest in the kingdom of heaven. . . . But if anyone causes one of these little ones who believe in me to sin, it would be better for him to have a large millstone hung around his neck and to be drowned in the depths of the sea."[2]

Jesus is so serious about being openhearted like a child that he says it would be better for someone to be killed instead of causing a child to close off his or her heart. This is especially true for men. When a man closes off his heart to the richness of adventure he was made to encounter in life, he grows dull and discontented—and there is no telling where this will come out.

We crave adventure. If we can't live it, we can sure purchase it. We'll buy it courtside or at a stadium. Or we'll take it free on television. And sports aren't the only way we satisfy our craving for adventure. We also crave adventure in our relationships, and when marriage feels mundane and dissatisfying, we turn our attention to the Internet, to magazines, or even to outside relationships to try to satisfy the hunger. "It is estimated that Americans now spend somewhere around $10 billion a year on adult entertainment, which is as much as they spend attending professional sporting events, buying music, or going out to the movies."[3] We are hungry for something, and we'll get the need met one way or another.

We're created to be warriors. We were made for battle. And

we get energized every time the opportunity is served up. We can get energized just by watching the battle played out in front of us. That's why millions of men check out of their regular lives on Sunday afternoons and Monday nights all across America. It's why billions of dollars are spent on sporting events every year. From 1953 to 2002, $20 billion of public money was spent on the construction of sports stadiums in the United States. This figure doesn't include the percentage that team owners and private donors contributed. And this money was just to get the stadiums built! It doesn't touch the amount of money we spent to see the games that were played in the stadiums.[4]

God designed men to be dangerous. Look at the imagination, dreams, and desires written into the heart of every boy: hero, warrior, and explorer. Sadly, most men abandon those dreams in favor of more obtainable and predictable avocations. The true heart of a man, what God designed us to be, is bent toward danger, passion, and freedom. Men are made to war against evil.

When men are engaged in watching or participating in sports, they are touching a vital part of their souls. Why else would educated, grown adults stand alone in a room, screaming fearlessly at a television set? We get swept up in the passion, the competition, the camaraderie, the battle, and the longing to be a part of something larger than ourselves.

When a woman calls a man away from the game, it brings him right back into reality. He's a middle-aged, overweight, has-been (or never-was), riding a leather La-Z-Boy instead of a wild bronco, holding a remote control instead of a sword and shield. "Can't it wait till halftime?" really means, "I'm at war right now, and I can't leave the battlefield."

SO, WHAT'S A WOMAN TO DO?

1. Adventure is written into the heart of a man. Invite him to experience risk. You do him a disservice when you stand in the way of his opportunity.
2. Examine where you are supportive and where you are not supportive of his having outlets for adventure.
3. You can never give a man enough of yourself to make up for what he is made to get from finding adventure with other men. You weren't made to fill that role, and he will resent you for it if you try.

5
"WANNA DO IT?"

WRITING IS A MIXED BAG for me (David). I really enjoy the feeling of accomplishment when a book is done, but it also means a lot of weekends away from my wife and kids. My three-year-old son recently commented to me as I headed out for the evening to write, "Dad, we already have lots of books. You don't need to write another one."

In addition to the time lost with my family, the cost for me can be measured in pounds. When I'm working on a manuscript, I can usually be found most weekends holed up at the Frothy Monkey, my favorite neighborhood coffee shop, enjoying a good cup of coffee and dessert while I write. As I attempt to crank out a few thousand words, I manage to take in a few hundred calories.

One Sunday evening, I had been tapping away on my laptop for a couple of hours when I noticed the owner of the Frothy

Monkey approaching me with a man who was new to the neighborhood. As they drew near, Miranda began introductions.

Maybe this guy's a writer, too, I thought, *or maybe he's interested in old houses and wants to inquire about the historical neighborhood.*

Instead, Miranda said, "This is Aaron, and he can't make up his mind whether to have the mocha pie or the mixed berry cobbler. I told him you had tried every dessert we ever made [several times] and could comment on any dessert in question."

I smiled, touched my soft, squishy stomach, and gave my endorsement to the mixed berry cobbler.

At home, later that evening, before I climbed into bed, I stepped onto the scale. As the arrow leaped toward the 200-pound mark, it occurred to me that with my latest writing project, I had somehow managed to put on the same amount of weight my wife had gained when carrying our twins. I was nothing but a sack of fat and cholesterol: a fleshy fanny pack of mocha pie, turtle cheesecake, white chocolate cappuccinos, mixed berry cobbler, dark chocolate torte with fresh raspberries, hazelnut lattes, and decadent brownies with ground pecans. How could this have happened?

I have always had a strong affection for food. Some might call it an addiction—and maybe it is, but I simply refer to it as a love affair. My wife loves to cook, and I love to eat. We were made for each other.

Okay, if the truth be told, it's more of a *passionate* love affair. It's not like I could take it or leave it. I really *love* to eat. I would last for maybe two days on *Survivor* before I would become volatile and profane.

Sometimes, when the waiter at a restaurant approaches my

table to introduce the specials, I get teary . . . noticeably emotional. Well-prepared food is in the same category as sex for me. I love it that much. I've been known to lose myself in the company of good food, unable to carry on a conversation with my fellow diners or form coherent sentences. I've humiliated my wife in public by eating off friends' plates who can't finish their meals. (As I write these words, I am becoming keenly aware that I meet the criteria for a food addiction. . . . I probably need to talk to someone about this.)

Not only do I love food, but it also comforts me. It soothes me. I grew up in the Deep South, so that's legal. My grandmother can prepare a meal that could make a person bow to an idol. Dining at her table is a religious experience.

Let's just leave it at this: Food gives me more pleasure than is healthy for a man of my height and stature. This would come as no surprise to anyone who saw me shortly after I turned in a manuscript. I'm certain that as Miranda escorted Aaron to my table that evening, he must have been thinking, *Yes, this man is well acquainted with the dessert menu here. I should listen.*

CUT TO THE CHASE

Pleasure is at the center of human existence. Men and women are hardwired to seek pleasure and avoid pain. For many guys, however, when it comes to pleasure seeking, they have tunnel vision. They get so focused on the result that they ignore the process. As the Danish philosopher Søren Kierkegaard put it, "Most men pursue pleasure with such breathless haste that they hurry past it." This is often true when it comes to sex. In their desires for pleasure and physical contact, men often become focused on the prize, talk becomes unnecessary, and they say stupid things like, "Wanna do it?"

To a woman, this sounds like nothing more than "let's get down to business." For her, it's all about the process; the pleasure begins with the quality of the relationship. She is likely craving intimacy and connection. He is likely craving pleasure and contact. As actor and comedian Billy Crystal says, "Women need a reason to have sex; men just need a place."

The notion of pleasure cannot be fully explored apart from an understanding of brain chemistry, psychology, and theology. Let's start with the head and move down to the heart.

IMPULSE AND INSTINCT

Scientists have recently begun to take another look at the neurochemistry of love, sex, and the experience of pleasure. The hub for these events is the limbic system, often referred to as the emotive center of the brain. This part of the brain plays host to emotions, impulses, drives, and desires. (In other words, this is where the disco ball is hung and the party takes place.)

One of the key components of sexuality in the limbic system is a neurotransmitter known as dopamine. In the "wanna-do-it dance," this is the chemical that spikes the party punch with Spanish fly. It activates the brain's reward center, the portion of the limbic system that drives nearly all human behavior. Dopamine is one of the body's "feel good" chemicals. Elevated levels of dopamine produce focused attention and unwavering motivation. Simply stated, the more dopamine in the system, the greater the reward. For most of us, our brains release a lot more dopamine when we have a piece of chocolate cake than if we have a cup of

Earl Grey tea. But what's interesting to consider is that it isn't so much the chocolate cake we crave; it's the dopamine rush. And the same is true when it comes to sex. Dopamine is the primary chemical released during orgasm.

For men, the "wanna-do-it dance" is connected to the desire for a dopamine rush. The typical male brain produces much more dopamine than the female brain.[1]

But female/male neurochemistry differs in other significant ways besides dopamine. Some of the more obvious differences occur with the hormone oxytocin, which is produced in much greater quantities in women than in men. It is sometimes referred to as the "cuddling" or "bonding" hormone. In the "wanna-do-it dance," it's the clingy girl in the corner who just wants to slow dance. Oxytocin is released when skin to skin touch occurs (unlike dopamine, which is released primarily during orgasm). How women's brains and men's brains deal with oxytocin is also quite different. Estrogen, the chief female hormone, enhances oxytocin's effect on mood and behavior. Estrogen is like oxytocin's little sister, who encourages bonding relationships. On the other hand, testosterone, the primary male hormone, counteracts the effects of oxytocin. Testosterone is the dumb jock of hormones. It's the man's man chemical.

All this brain chemistry information can be overwhelming. Dopamine, oxytocin, estrogen, and testosterone are just a few of the players in a very complex set of chemical interactions, and hundreds of scientific articles and books have been written on the subject. But by barely scratching the surface, we can see that the differences in brain chemistry between men and women really do influence who we are and how we relate with each other. There is a biological cause for every biological event, but even though neurochemistry can help to explain what is happening between our ears, it isn't the only factor when the question of "wanna do it?" rises to the surface.

SEX, THE HEART, AND THE SOUL

Maybe it's because I (Stephen) am trained as a counselor, maybe it's because I'm a pastor in a church, or maybe it's because I'm left-handed, but for whatever reason, sometimes people I hardly know disclose things to me that would be inappropriate or awkward any other time. Casual acquaintances are willing to bring up things they wouldn't normally talk about, even things I have zero knowledge or training in. Like the guy I met on an airplane (Larry, a textile salesman, I think he said) who, after I told him I was a counselor, proceeded to ask me for advice about his family dog. He wanted to teach Barney, a toy poodle, how to do tricks like fetching, begging, and rolling over.

"Well, like I said," I replied patiently, "I work mostly with couples and individuals. I don't really know that much about pets."

"But you know about that Pavlov guy, right?" Larry persisted. "I saw something about him on the History Channel. He was kind of a psychologist, wasn't he? He trained those dogs with the bell, right?"

"Well, sure, I studied Pavlov in grad school. But I think he was more of a behavioral scientist. I'm not sure that he really did a lot of counseling. That's what I do." Still trying to get him to understand that I couldn't really help him with his dog, I said, "Larry, I work with *people* on things like depression or marriage problems—issues like that."

"Do any of those people have dogs?" Larry asked. By this point, I was wondering whether he was simply pulling my leg. I kind of chuckled to myself and tried to politely change the subject with my new friend.

"Larry, tell me what you do. Do you travel much? Do you like your job?" I thought these questions would surely distract him from his concerns about Barney. And for a while they did. Larry told me about the rigors of business travel and his long career as a salesman. Meanwhile, the flight attendant brought us our beverages and peanuts.

As Larry took a drink of his Diet Coke and munched his peanuts, he mumbled, "Back to Barney. How can I make him obey?"

After trying again and again to explain my work as a counselor, but with Larry not relenting, I finally gave in and made a suggestion. "Well, have you tried teaching Barney by *demonstrating* the commands to him? Like, if you want him to sit, you sit on the floor in front of him. If you want him to beg, you show him how to do it. Things like that." All the while, Larry nodded attentively. I still get a chuckle imagining this chubby textile salesman in front of his toy poodle, showing him how to fetch, beg, and roll over.

Sometimes, however, this openness that people feel to share things with me results in some really honest and painful conversations. Like the time I met Karen and Eric through a mutual friend. Before long, they were talking to me about the state of their marriage, and they both expressed some frustration. "Like what?" I asked, naively thinking it would be something about how he works too much, or something of that nature.

Eric looked at his wife and then back to me. "We've been married for a little more than a year, and we don't have sex anymore."

"Oh."

Eric went on to tell me that it had been months since he and Karen had been sexual in any way—and really, they'd had sex very little since the first few weeks of their relationship. "This lack of intimacy is really beginning to negatively affect our marriage," Eric lamented.

"Mm-hmm."

It was evident that Karen and Eric loved each other very much. They were an attractive, outgoing, intelligent couple, who were so hungry for something different in their marriage that they were willing to talk with a stranger about the deepest shame in their relationship. I reassured them that their situation was not uncommon, and that many couples have been in the same place they were. (I also knew that although this line of reasoning might help to comfort them and ease their shame, it would do little to assist them with their problem.)

In an effort to be helpful, I asked them if they'd be willing to tell me a little bit more about their relationship. This time, Karen spoke. "Ever since we've been married," she began sadly, "whenever we're alone, Eric makes some kind of sexual advance. He gropes at me or he makes these sexual innuendoes all the time. A backrub can never be just a backrub . . . we can't ever *just* cuddle. I'm never beautiful or lovely to him. I'm always 'hot' or 'sexy.' But the worst is when we're watching TV or a movie, and he blurts out something like, 'Wanna do it?' It makes me feel so cheap, like . . . like . . . like a whore."

Karen and Eric are not alone in their feelings of alienation from each other. They are like the 71 percent of couples who have been together ten years or more and are dissatisfied with their sex life.[2] Many couples express similar sentiments.

WRONGHEADED THINKING ABOUT SEX

The more that David and I talk with people (both in and out of our counseling offices), the more we realize that many people have wrong ideas about sex. They're confused about the proper role of sex in their relationships, and these flawed views lead to all kinds of resentment, shame, and conflict. We've found that these flawed ways of thinking boil down into six general categories: fabrication, miscommunication, recreation, masturbation, affirmation, and compensation.

FABRICATION

The fabrication perspective views sex primarily as the means to an end; that is, sex is designed for making babies. Though procreation can certainly be an end result, it's far from what most people want to be the center of their sex lives. When this category is the primary perspective of sex, it ultimately leads to shame for both men and women. The success or failure to achieve conception becomes the measuring stick. *Did we make a baby? Are we pregnant? Did it work this time?* Sex becomes pressure filled. Ultimately, women end up treating their bodies as machines for conceiving, growing, and nurturing babies, and men become sexual civil servants—like firemen—on call and ready to jump into action at the ring of the ovulatory bell. Though fabrication can initially be energizing for couples, it usually ends up in fatigue and shame if it goes on for any length of time. Sex becomes just one more thing on the to-do list.

MISCOMMUNICATION

Through sex, men and women can communicate and experience things that cannot be put into words. That's true. Sex can be a means through which a man and a woman can transcend their differences and articulate their care and love for each another. But this connection is more of a by-product of sex than a designed objective. Too often, men and women use sex as a way of avoiding difficult conversations, or it becomes a way of resolving conflict. For many couples, sex is a haven of artificial intimacy in the midst of a dysfunctional relationship. Sex becomes a substitute for doing the hard work of communicating. Similarly, what is often called "makeup sex" is a shortcut around the labor of coming to authentic resolution. Sex becomes a way of manufacturing trust that has been eroded by conflict, without ever having to enter your spouse's pain, say you're sorry, or alter the way you act toward him or her.

RECREATION

Another popular view of sex is that it's primarily for recreation. As with procreation and miscommunication, there's an element of truth here. Sex can be a lot of fun. Without a doubt, it must be pleasurable if it is to bring life and intimacy to a relationship. But holding onto the idea that sex is primarily for entertainment is damaging to a relationship in the long run. The recreation view of sex robs us of the mystery and majesty that is central to what sex is really all about. It also overlooks the power and depth of what sexual intimacy can bring to a relationship. Though we don't have to go to the opposite extreme and view sex as an ultraserious experience, when we see it as principally a recreational enterprise, it trivializes and ignores the power and spiritual significance of a man and a woman joining their bodies as one.

MASTURBATION

Many people approach sex from an entirely selfish perspective. At its core, sex is designed to be a relational endeavor between a man and a woman. But whenever someone puts his or her own interests above those of the spouse, sex becomes *anti*-relational. Self-interested sex, which in essence depersonalizes the other person, is really nothing more than mutual masturbation. Sex, which is designed to be a deeply shared experience, ends in loneliness, withdrawal, and shame. It's not uncommon for husbands and wives to approach sex with self-interest as their primary motive. And even if they satisfy their physical needs, the sexual experience will have fallen well short of what it was designed to be.

AFFIRMATION

A lot of people use sex as a way of validating their self-worth. They look to sex for affirmation and to answer the question, "Am I okay?" This approach to sex is most common among men, but women are not immune to this way of thinking. Men often turn to their wives after sex and want to know if they've done a good job—is she satisfied? Men who tend to do this are usually insecure and fearful. They doubt themselves in the relationship. This is why many women find these kinds of questions a huge turnoff. Typically, by asking questions designed to affirm his own self-image, a man squelches his relationship with his wife by putting her on the spot and causing her embarrassment or shame. Questions like "How was it?" or "Did you enjoy yourself?" reduce sex to a graded performance and thereby eliminate the intimacy that is more central to what sex is really all about.

COMPENSATION

One of the more damaging views of sex is that it is a reward. Whereas men are more prone to use sex for affirmation, some women are guilty of using sex as a means of compensation. In many relationships, sex becomes a payoff for good behavior. Some men, but mostly women, play scorekeeper in hopes that they'll get their other emotional needs met. A man once complained to me (Stephen) in counseling, "It feels like she has this secret list, and until I accomplish everything on it, we won't have sex. The thing is, I don't know what's on the list, but I know it's long. It's like she has me held hostage." When sex is used as compensation, it usually leads to resentment for both men and women. This view of sex as reward is destructive to trust and wreaks havoc on intimacy.

UNCOVERING THE MYSTERY

Here is some good news: Sex is a profound and powerful mystery created by God to reveal his glory, express his character, and please his creation. Yet we're like children in our understanding of what sex is really about and how it all works. We struggle to understand its true purpose and design.

Recently, some close friends of mine (David's) delivered their second child, and I took my kids to meet the new arrival. On our way to the hospital, I retold all three of my children the stories of their own births. I should have known what I was getting myself into.

From the back of the car, my little girl asked, "How did the doctor get me out of Mommy's tummy?" I responded with, "Well, that's a great question." What I was actually thinking was, *Oh crap! Where's Connie?* I had no intention of educating our children on the nature of labor and delivery at this age.

Before I had a chance to answer the question, one of my four-year-olds answered by saying, "He pulled you out of Mommy's belly button."

My daughter snapped back, "No he didn't, Witt. Your belly button is closed, and nothing goes in or comes out."

My other son offered his explanation. "I think they cut Mommy's tummy open and pulled us out quick and put a zipper on and zipped it back together."

Lily argued, "Mommy doesn't have a zipper on her tummy, Baker. And she doesn't have a scar from a cut place."

I stepped into the banter before they began speculating on how the baby got *into* Mommy's tummy. "Lily, you're right. Mommy does not have a zipper or a scar on her tummy because none of you came out of her tummy. But some babies do, and that's called a C-section. It's one way of delivering a baby. The doctor just makes a small cut in the mommy's tummy and pulls the baby right out."

My daughter pressed forward. "So how did I come out?"

"Well, you came out of . . . of . . . of . . . of . . . Mommy's vagina," I said with some reluctance.

She began laughing and said, "No, I didn't. Only pee pee comes out your vagina. Silly Daddy!"

"I know that does sound silly, and usually pee pee is the only thing that comes out, but after nine months of pregnancy, God makes a woman's body ready by making her vagina stretch so a baby can come out." (At this point, I'm thinking, *If she asks one more question about the vagina, I'm going to hand her the cell phone to call her mother*.)

My sons were pretty quiet at this point, until one of them spoke up and said, "Well, how did we get *inside* Mommy's tummy?" (I started freaking out because I had thought I had at least another four or five years to prepare for this one.)

I remembered that the week before, on vacation, we had seen some baby sea turtles hatch, crawl out of their hole in the sand, and waddle to the ocean. I decided that was all the information I was giving. "Well, you remember the baby sea turtles from the beach? How they were inside a little egg and then they hatched and crawled out? You came from a little egg and then made your way out." I didn't skip a breath and then said, "How about Mexican food after we go to the hospital? We haven't had chicken fajitas or verde salsa in a long time."

Just as my children believed that babies exited through the belly button, and I had no clue how to respond to their questions at that moment, most people don't understand how it all *really* works. We tend to live with a limited view of the design and purpose for sex, when there is so much more to it. In many respects, sex is a profoundly mysterious spiritual experience. It is also one of the strongest innate physical drives. At its purest, sex reveals the heart of God and connects us to our spouses at the deepest level.

There are at least six aspects of sexual expression that we

must consider if we want to understand what God intended when he designed this weird and wonderful facet of human interaction: procreation, revelation, gratification, adoration, unification, and transformation.

PROCREATION

Understanding the procreative aspect of sex is completely different from seeing the purpose of sex as mere fabrication. It moves beyond the idea of "well, we've been married a while, and I guess the next natural step is to get pregnant," to seeing the biblical calling of multiplying and filling the earth. Procreation is our opportunity to join God in the act of creation—the creation of life. New life brings renewed hope and renewed joy, and it reminds us of God's presence.

REVELATION

God made our bodies with the potential for making the invisible visible. We are "cast in flesh" in order to uncover the mystery of an unseen God. We're not merely spiritual beings; we are incarnated. In our bodies, and especially through our sexuality, there is a promise that points to God's glory. God is personified in our sexuality.

Perhaps you're saying, "There is no way my body reveals God's glory," but that's not how God sees it. When he wanted to make aspects of his invisible nature visible to us, he stamped his image into our embodied beings, creating us as male and female.[3]

We're all familiar with the line often spoken at weddings: "A man will leave his father and mother and join with his wife, and the two will become one flesh." This line comes from the Bible and is first used in the book of Genesis to explain marriage, in reference to Adam and Eve.[4] From the very beginning of humankind, God used sex between husbands and wives as an expression of the divine nature. One of the best pictures we get of God's relationship with us is that of a husband and wife joined, intertwined, and combined in a "one flesh" relationship.

The two coming together to make one flesh is reflective of the Holy Trinity, a perfect companionship of three beings: God the Father (creator and sustainer); God the Son (redeemer and savior); and God the Spirit (power and presence). Likewise, as human beings, we are created primarily for relationship. We understand ourselves only through our relationships with God and with one another.

The apostle Paul calls all this leaving and joining and making one flesh a "profound mystery." In his letter to the community of Christ-followers living in the ancient town of Ephesus, Paul specifically uses the relationship of a man and a woman "becoming one flesh" as an image of Jesus' relationship with his people (the church).[5]

GRATIFICATION

If we are to have an accurate view of sex as God intended it, we cannot overlook the truth that sex is for pleasure—not pleasure solely, but pleasure nonetheless. Sex is designed for enjoyment—for both husbands and wives. It results in a mutual "Yes!" and a simultaneous "Thank you!" Sex is gratifying, life-giving, and revitalizing.

In a world poisoned with heartache, death, and decay, sex is a powerful antidote to despair. Embedded within our sexuality is the very real possibility that we can transcend our physical limitations, move beyond mere recreational enjoyment, and discover deep, soul-level gratification. Orgasm is the moment when we're most fully aware of ourselves and—at the same time—outside of ourselves. Sexual climax embodies a pleasure paradox. At the point of our greatest enjoyment, we are simultaneously full and empty, all-together satisfied and yet wanting, at once fulfilled and yet disappointed. True pleasure always brings an ache for that "something more" that cannot be fulfilled this side of heaven. The pleasure of sex gives us a taste of eternity. Gratification includes at least the seeds of a God-given desire for more. In a biblical sense, gratification satisfies us deeply, while at the same time pointing us toward a day when we will be satisfied (and sanctified) completely.

ADORATION

Sex is worship—which is one reason why it's important not to take it too lightly or ignore it. Depending on your background, it may seem odd, sacrilegious, or downright pagan to equate sex with worship. But that's only because we have separated our understanding of sex from our knowledge of God. We need to better understand how sex reflects how we worship.

As God's image bearers, we are made to worship. As such, we are worshiping all the time. The only question is *what* are we worshiping? We're either worshiping God or something else. In that context, then, sex is either an expression of adoration to God, or it's a corruption of what God intended.

Gratitude combines our recognition of having received

more than we ever deserved, given freely without obligation, and our awareness of that gift. Gratitude, when fully realized, always leads to awe.

Awe is the jaw-dropping moment when we run out of words, or when we throw back our heads and say "Wow!" or "Yes!" When we are stunned by the beauty of it all and experience a profound sense of humility. When we are in the presence of something bigger than ourselves that is beautiful, powerful, and awesome. We are designed to be caught up into that which is bigger, all-pervading, and supreme. We really, really like this.

When gratitude and awe collide, it sounds something like this: "Oh God, thank you! Yes! Wow! Oh God, thank you!" That sounds a lot like sex, doesn't it? But what we're describing here is worship. Now, that's weird.

UNIFICATION

Sex brings people together. It fosters intimacy. Scripture doesn't say that "the two just shared in each other's flesh." It says, "For this reason a man will leave his father and mother and be united to his wife, and they will become one flesh."[6] Sex is an expression of unification, a joining together for the purpose of creating deeper intimacy—the giving over of a man to a woman and a woman to a man. Sex is the acknowledgement that every part of us—body, mind, and soul—is being offered to another person as an act of unity.

Consider how sharing in something sacred, whether triumphant, tragic, or mundane, joins us with other people. Fighting in war together, being in the delivery room with your spouse at the first sign of your newborn, losing a parent to death, being part of a cultural tragedy or natural disaster—walking through events like these binds people together in relationship. How much more so in the glorious act of sex shared between two people as a holy and sacred expression of love. Sex, through this kind of expression, is a physical, emotional, and spiritual joining of two bodies, two hearts, and two souls.

TRANSFORMATION

Sex is meant to change us. Biologically, sex alters our biochemistry. Relationally, sex changes our marriage relationships. Spiritually, it can reveal the divine and lead us toward worship. Sex is intended by God to be an experience that transforms us into different people.

If we have experienced sexuality in ways that are outside of God's design or hope for our lives, we are familiar with the downside of sex—the shame, self-loathing, and contempt that can accompany sex. That's why sex can be so difficult. That's why people sometimes wander away mentally during sex or fantasize about someone else or wish for it to just hurry up and end. Because of past shame and hurt, we become unavailable, inattentive, or absent from the moment (like daydreaming in the middle of a sermon or daydreaming about a sermon during sex).

Think of your own life. Not just your sex life—all of your life. Are you present to the experience? Are you really there, or are you trying to get away from the moment? Are you moving away to escape something? Is your life full of "if" statements? *If this hadn't happened, life would be . . .* ; or, *If I had done . . . , then I wouldn't be . . .* ; or, *If I could ever get to this certain point, then life would be okay*. Do you avoid life in the present by being a prisoner to the past or fleeing into the future?

In order for life to be what it is intended to be, you have to be present. Being present means bringing all of who you are to the moment: all your memories, all your longings, all your heartache, all your faith, all your hopes, all your dreams. When it comes to sex, most of us are not truly present. We live stagnant lives—inside and outside the bedroom.

Transformed living invites us to bring all of ourselves to the present moment—both the sinner and the saint. Though we constantly need to be forgiven, we never forfeit our distinctive dignity as God's image bearers. Of course, bringing all of who we are into our daily life experiences (let alone into the bedroom) is far bigger than most of us can imagine, because exposing all of who we are reveals our incompleteness, our need for God and for others, our need for forgiveness, and our need for redemption. But if we can ever be fully present, in our needs, our hopes, and our desires, it will open us to an experience of life that is bigger and more amazing than we can imagine.

On the other hand, when we are unable to bring all of who we are to the moment (sexually or otherwise), at some level we dissociate from life and from our true design. We separate ourselves from a present availability to other people (and to God). Dissociation or disconnection *feels* like a very safe place to be, because to be present is to be profoundly out of control (especially if we bring all of our desires and hopes to the moment). But when we fail to bring all of who we are to relational moments (such as sex), we end up walking away from the moment with some level of shame and contempt. We all face the temptation or impulse to rein ourselves in. But when we hold back, we commit ourselves to some level of disappointment—and we come to expect it.

Internally—and perhaps subconsciously—we say things like, "I'll let you touch me, but I won't let myself enjoy it."

Presence is a willingness to be vulnerable. If we're not willing to risk being hurt, we will not be open to receiving—or giving—a blessing. Ask yourself: Are you willing to be caught off guard, to be out of control? Being present exposes both our dignity and our depravity, our virtues and our vices. This is true intimacy—and for the most part, we don't want it. We don't want to be seen with quite so much clarity.

Through transformation, however, sex offers us a redemptive experience. If we can learn to make ourselves fully known to our spouses—if we can take the risk of genuine intimacy, we can vanquish shame, self-loathing, and contempt, which become faint shadows in the light of our glory.

This is how God intended for sex to be—transformative, healing, sustaining, and nurturing. Through intimacy, authenticity, and integrity in our marriage relationships, sex can bring us to greater maturity, wisdom, and holiness because it affords us the chance to live with freedom from shame. God designed sex as a way of giving us hope. Sex is designed to be a relational act between husbands and wives that transcends biology and transports us into the unseen realm of God's glory.

Sex, as designed by God, is intended to reveal his glory. Thus, all sexual expression comes down to a simple question: Does this behavior incarnate God's love and glory, or does it not? We know it sounds a bit lofty, but it's not that complicated . . . is it? When a man asks, "Wanna do it?" it's at some level an invitation to worship and at some level an invitation to idolatry.

So, wanna do it?

SO, WHAT'S A WOMAN TO DO?

1. Honestly assess your views of sex. How closely do they align with the flawed categories presented earlier in the chapter?
2. Tell your husband or wife you'd like to dialogue more freely and frequently about the role of sex in your relationship.
3. In what areas of your life are you failing to bring all of who you are to your relational moments? How do you hide?

6
"YOUR PROBLEM IS..."

WHEN PEOPLE COME TO TALK with me (Stephen) at work, sooner or later they ask the same question: "Is *this* your office?"

"Yes."

"Well, where's your desk? Where do you do your work?"

"Being with *you* is my work," I usually say. "This is what I do. I talk with people."

At this point, depending on the person, they either look grateful and relieved, or rigid and defensive. If I'm in the mood to have some fun, I may throw in an overtly psychological or analytical question, such as, "Does it bother you that I don't have a desk?" or "What does that make you feel?"

I love my job.

I have nothing against desks. It's just that my office isn't very big, and because the majority of my work is centered on having conversations with people, I have little need for a desk. However, I do have an armoire along one wall, which houses my laptop, the phone, a few files, and (currently) stacks of DVDs. When I do spend time at my computer, the doors to the armoire envelop me like a sarcophagus. It's kind of creepy, now that I think about it.

So there I was one afternoon, entombed in my armoire. I'd been in meetings all day and had only about twenty minutes before my next appointment. I was furiously checking e-mail and trying to return phone calls when I heard my silenced cell phone buzzing in my messenger's bag on the floor next to me. I carelessly rifled through the bag to find the phone.

(Here's a random aside: I'm a little weird when it comes to bags. I have probably three times as many bags as my wife has purses. No, really, it's true. Backpacks, sling packs, briefcases, day packs, messenger's bags—you name it, I've got it. I do, however, avoid fanny packs. For me, bags spark romantic notions of adventure and exploration. I secretly daydream of being like MacGyver from the old TV show—kind of a cross between Sheriff Andy Taylor and Indiana Jones. But don't be confused; these are not "man purses." It's all manly, rugged gear. But I digress . . .)

On this day when my phone rang, I was carrying a very well-constructed, oversized, black-and-cobalt-blue Trager messenger's bag with a padded laptop case. With so many useful compartments, I had trouble finding the phone before it stopped vibrating. When it finally turned up, I looked at the caller ID to see whose call I had missed. Seeing that it was my wife, I casually dialed her back, tucked the phone between my ear and shoulder, and kept skimming my e-mails.

"Hello?" Heather said.

"Hey, honey. How's it going? Sorry I missed your call. I couldn't get to my phone."

"What are you doing?" she asked.

"Nothing. I am just between appointments and was checking e-mail when you called." I could hear an emotional ruckus in the background. "It sounds pretty crazy on your end. What's going on?"

"*Your* sons refused to take a nap today, so now they're cranky and throwing temper tantrums." (Our youngest, the twins, were about eight months old at the time.) At this point, I should have recognized that something was really wrong and Heather was at the end of her rope. Anytime your wife refers to the kids as *yours,* it's a clue that something negative is happening. Now, any husband with a modicum of insight into marriage would've known to close the laptop and listen to his wife. But, of course, I'm not just *any* husband.

"That's nice," I said, typing away at an e-mail.

"You're not even listening!" Heather said. "What are you doing? Answering your e-mail?" *This wasn't the first time I had only half-listened when she called.*

Like an idiot I said, "No, I'm listening," and I gently pleaded with her to tell me what was going on.

"I told you," she replied, her voice mixed with anger, desperation, and exhaustion. Whatever she had originally called about was now irrelevant. Her problem was now with me.

Suddenly realizing that I had failed to hold up my end of the dialogue, I scrambled to reconstruct the conversation in my head to find a point where I could salvage whatever credibility I had left.

"Who's crying?" I asked.

"It's the twins. They're freaking out."

"Did they get their nap?" (Yes, I am *that* stupid.)

"Obviously you're too busy," Heather said. "I've got to go handle this." And she hung up.

Being the caring guy that I am, I immediately called her back. "Hey, I'm sorry I wasn't paying attention. What's going on?"

"The twins are being a royal pain. They won't stop screaming. I've tried everything I know to do. I have to leave in ten minutes to run afternoon carpool and then make everyone's dinner. Then Emma Claire has a project due tomorrow that she hasn't finished yet." Heather's anger was melting into heartache. "When can you come home?"

"I can't leave for a couple more hours. I have two appointments. Have you tried letting them have a snack?" I offered.

"They just finished lunch."

"What about holding them?"

"I've been holding them all day."

"Can they play outside in their playpen?" I was running low on solutions and was starting to get anxious.

"It's about to rain, and like I told you, I have to go get the kids from school. Never mind. I have to go. I'll just see you later."

"I'm sorry it's so hard. What can I do to help?"

"I've got to go."

"I'll call you on my way home. Hey, what are we doing for dinner?"

"Good-bye, Stephen, okay?"

"Okay. I love you. Bye."

Click. She hung up.

I dropped my head and leaned into my office-in-a-box, thinking, *Wow, that went badly.*

Now, this is a pretty extreme example from my marriage, and to my credit, I'm nowhere near this absurdly oblivious most of the time. But even though it isn't always this rough, more often than I will admit I have missed entire phone conversations with Heather because I was trying to multitask.

In this situation, what my wife needed more than anything was for me to empathize with her. She needed me, to the best of my ability, to join her in her plight. She was tired, lonely, and hurt. She needed me to listen, hear her out, and be with her. Instead, I offered solutions. She needed compassion. I supplied resolution. She longed for consideration. I provided answers. She desired me to get in it with her. I gave her outcomes.

USER ERROR

How is it that men can so completely miss connecting with women? Why, in the face of heartache, do men try to fix women's problems instead of just empathizing with them? The answer lies in how we were made. (Bear with us here. A little bit of background is in order.)

When God created Eve and presented her to Adam, the very first words he spoke to them together were a blessing:

"Be fruitful and increase in number; fill the earth and subdue it. Rule over the fish of the sea and the birds of the air and over every living creature that moves on the ground."[1]

God gave the man and the woman everything on the entire earth as a gift. In essence, he said, "Go make love and have babies.

Everything is for you. Take care of it, enjoy it, pay attention to it, and get life from it."

Wow! It's like God is the ultimate sugar daddy.

In dedicating Adam and Eve to accomplish two explicit purposes—filling and multiplying, and subduing and ruling—God revealed to them how they would find their greatest fulfillment and blessing. As they pursued their mission, they would reflect the nature of their Creator. In the Genesis account, God spent six days filling and multiplying and subduing and ruling the earth. Then he turned the responsibility over to humankind. Just like Adam and Eve, we reflect the image of God and are most like we were created to be when we function as creators and stewards, artists and guardians. We are most like we were designed to be when we create and govern together.

"Who cares?" you say. "Where are you going with all this? Why do men try to fix women's problems?" Hold on. It's coming.

Looking at the two directives (filling and multiplying, and subduing and ruling), we see some obvious differences. One is creative, and the other is administrative. One is more graceful; the other more forceful. One is more tender; the other stronger. We might even say that one is more feminine and the other is more masculine. This harmony of might and mercy is part of the nature of God that we, as men and women, are intended to reflect. As it says in the Psalms, "Power belongs to you, God, and with you, Lord, is unfailing love."[2]

The prophet Zephaniah also captures the essence of God's might and mercy:

> The LORD your God is with you,
> the Mighty Warrior who saves.

He will take great delight in you;
in his love he will no longer rebuke you,
but will rejoice over you with singing.[3]

Zephaniah's imagery evokes both a warrior-liberator (think William Wallace in *Braveheart*) and a mother holding her child, singing a lullaby. Other passages, such as Isaiah 42, speak of God simultaneously as a triumphant combatant and a woman crying, panting, and gasping in childbirth.[4] These are excellent expressions of God's might and mercy, which are reflected in the essential characteristics of men (warrior combatant) and women (nurturing mother).

We're not suggesting that women don't have strength or that men don't have tenderness. But a woman who is fully herself and expressing the image of God will be tenderly strong. And a man who is fully himself and expressing the image of God will be strongly tender. To be a woman is to have a heart bent for relationship. To be a man is to have a heart bent for war.

But when things went wrong in the Garden of Eden (and not all that differently from how things go wrong in our relationships today), Adam and Eve betrayed, blamed, and lied to each other and God, and brought consequences on themselves.[5] What's interesting about the consequences described in Genesis 3 is that they are specifically tied to each sex's unique characteristics. The curse for women is different from the curse for men.

For women, the curse strikes at the center of their relationships, through loneliness.[6] For men, it strikes at their sense of competency, through failure.[7] Does that mean a woman can't feel like a failure or that a man can't be lonely? Of course not.

But for women, the primary experience of the curse will be *relational* (creation, fertility, and loneliness), whereas for men, it will be *vocational* (exertion, futility, and decay). For women, no relationship will be enough. For men, everything they do will be hard and will fall apart.

MRS. FEEL IT MEETS MR. FIX IT

Okay, so what does all this have to do with men trying to fix women's problems? Here's a little case study.

A woman comes to her husband after a painful falling-out with her closest friend at work. She is tearful and feels abandoned and betrayed. Part of her heart has been torn out. She's understandably crying and confused: her face in her hands, snot dripping from her nose, her complexion blotchy with emotion. She looks up to her husband with a look that says, "Help me. Please." He responds with something like, "Here's what I think you should do . . ."

Now, you don't have to be Dr. Phil to figure out that this marriage is not working. So what's going on? Why is it that many men fail to know how to be helpful in situations like this?

I (David) recall sitting at a Ford dealership in Orlando, Florida, while on "vacation" with my wife and kids. (Once you have kids, the word *vacation* takes on new meaning.) We travel to Florida twice a year to be with my wife's family. We typically fly when we go, but this particular year, Southwest Airlines didn't have any deals on flights to Orlando, and we had just purchased a new SUV, so we hit the road.

According to Mapquest, we would travel 691 miles from our front door to our destination. Traveling 691 miles by automobile with my kids would translate into approximately twenty-two hours on the road. The average person could probably drive to Canada and back in the same amount of time it would take us to get from Nashville to Orlando.

Our plan was to travel halfway on Christmas evening, get a hotel, and finish the trip on December 26. It was a really good plan—*on paper*. The only minor setback on day one of our trip was a cold and cough that one of my sons had developed sometime on Christmas Day. Not a problem. We stopped at a gas station, picked up some cough medicine, and gave him a nightcap before bedtime at the hotel.

Early on day two, my other son started with similar symptoms. It was still not a major setback. We had plenty of cough syrup to get us through the week. We arrived in Orlando as planned, but we spent the next day holed up in our hotel room (my daughter having now come down with the sickness). By day four, the colds were worse and seemed more like pneumonia. I had made one trip to a local pediatrician and five trips to Walgreens for antibiotics, Kleenex, steroids, a thermometer, more cough syrup, a decongestant, one cool-air humidifier, cherry-flavored cough lozenges (not grape . . . I accidentally got grape on trip three and had to go back), more Kleenex, a warm-mist vaporizer, a nebulizer, and a partridge in a pear tree.

The whole experience was extremely disappointing to my kids, because my in-laws had found an amazing place for the whole family to stay just ten minutes from Disney World. Here it was four days into our Christmas vacation, and we had not so much as laid eyes on Mickey Mouse ("or Buzz Lightyear," cried my youngest son).

It was a rough start to the trip, but the worst was yet to come.

After dinner on day five, I decided we'd been trapped inside long enough. "We need to get out and get some fresh air," I announced to everyone. So we took a trip down International Drive and made a stop for ice cream. My five-year-old daughter had her first banana split. And despite the coughing, hacking, and all the runny noses, we seemed to be in our best spirits yet. (And let's be truthful, you can't help but feel better with a Dairy Queen Blizzard.)

I remember the drive back to the hotel. I remember there was a lot of traffic, but I drove with a sense of satisfaction. *Good idea, David. See, we just needed to get out for a while.* I only vaguely remember what came next, because I've tried to block it out of my memory. I believe it started with my daughter saying from the back seat, "Mommy, I feel sick." She had barely gotten the words out of her mouth when I remember hearing my wife scream, "Oh my God, drive fast! Lily is throwing up."

I looked into the rear view mirror, all the way back to the third row, and I could see my wife's jacket splashed in vomit. My daughter was leaning over, throwing up again on the floorboard of our *brand new* Ford Expedition. We're talking partially digested bananas, hot fudge sauce, pineapple, strawberries, and soft-serve ice cream. (And let me tell you, there is something about milk products in vomit that no one should have to endure.)

One of my three-year-old boys started crying a sympathy cry. There was really no reason for him to be sad, he just didn't want his sister to be crying alone. (Besides, you don't get any attention when you're quiet.) His crying turned to screaming when Lily's projectile vomit shot him squarely in the back of the head.

As my mother-in-law tried to soothe my son, my father-in-law took off his jacket and handed it over the seat back to my wife. I'm not really sure why he did this. It could have been used to catch more barf, to wipe down the third row of our *brand new* vehicle, to shield and protect my wife from projectile vomit, or to suffocate my screaming son. I personally wanted to use it as a parachute—to jump out of the car and off a bridge.

We made it back to the hotel in record time, and I screeched into the parking lot to unload my family. I lifted my sad, sick, covered-in-vomit little girl from the back seat. Actually, I slid her out. By this point, it was like a slip-and-slide from the third row of our *brand new* car to the second-row door. My wife slid out next. She, too, was covered in multicolored vomit. It was in her hair, all over her clothes, and somehow even down her back. By this time, both boys were screaming, and I was about ready to start screaming myself. It seemed like the only thing to do.

After we got the kids up to the room, my father-in-law and I spent the next hour outside in the parking lot, cleaning puke out of the back two rows. We made another trip to Walgreens—this time for Woolite Tough Stain, Arm and Hammer Carpet Fresh, Febreze Interior Spring Scent, four calling birds, three French hens, and two turtledoves. Meanwhile, Connie and her mother were bathing my daughter, soothing the boys, and trying to get everyone to sleep.

My wife and I spent the next seven hours helping Lily run to the bathroom to finish out the stomach virus, giving breathing treatments to my sons, wiping noses, and listening to all-night coughing. (I've never smoked pot, but that would have been the night to try it.) We also waited for the stomach virus to work its way through our family. (We have an almost perfect track record of passing a stomach virus from one family member to the next about two or three times a year. We are all about sharing.)

The next day, I walked down to the parking lot to take a look at the car. I had cleaned it in the dark the night before, and it felt important to survey the damage in the daylight. When I opened the door, I was overwhelmed by the stench. Despite eight rounds of Tough Stain, Carpet Fresh, and Febreze, the smell of puke was fresh and intense.

My mother-in-law mentioned that a friend of hers had put coffee grounds in her car to kill an intense smell, and it worked. So, we poured on several bowls of fresh ground coffee and drove around for the next two days enduring the sour smell.

Forty-eight more hours passed, and only two more people got the stomach virus, so we decided to venture out again. (What did we have to lose at this point?)

I made another one of my announcements: "This is getting ridiculous. We are minutes away from Disney World, and we've been trapped indoors for days on end. We're not leaving Orlando until we at least ride the monorail." (In retrospect, these are my thoughts: *What were you thinking? The monorail? Just declare defeat, man! Get back in your smelly, brand new car and drive home!*) I guess I just got stir-crazy and started hallucinating.

Somehow, I sold everyone on my foolish plan. It was probably due to their impaired mental faculties from dehydration. We loaded up, headed out, and I drove to the gates of glory to drop off my wife, her parents, and the kids. I proceeded toward the parking lot to park among the millions of other cars, and as I rolled down the window to receive my parking instructions from the guard, something strange happened. The window began grinding in slow motion as it lowered. I took the ticket and attempted to roll up the window. This time, it just made a grinding sound with no movement. I tried lowering the window again . . . just grinding. Again I tried to raise it . . . the same grinding—only worse now—until I heard the glass drop into the frame of the door and shatter.

At this point, I am thinking to myself, *I've been Punk'd!* The camera guy is going to come running out in just a minute, and people will be laughing. I'll be ticked, but it's all just a joke.

Instead, my wife called me on my cell phone to say, "Where are you? We are standing here waiting for you."

"Honey, you won't believe what I am about to tell you." I described what had just taken place, and of course she assumed I was joking. Then I said, "I'm scared to leave the car in the lot for fear that someone will take the stereo or the DVD player, or try to hot-wire the car." She reminded me that even if someone attempted to steal the car, they would be so disgusted by the smell of vomit and stale coffee that they'd surely just take the electronics and leave the car on the side of the road. She was right, so I left the car as it was and headed into Disney World.

The problem, however, was that I couldn't seem to shake the memory of broken glass and my exposed vehicle (my *brand new* car) sitting in the parking lot just waiting for a predator. I made the mistake (the *huge* mistake) of mentioning my concerns to my wife.

"Connie, I think I need to leave, go find a dealership, and fix the broken window. I've got to get this taken care of before we leave town tomorrow."

She looked at me with confusion and mild disdain, but said

kindly, "Honey, we haven't even been here an hour. We worked really hard to get everyone here. Let's just try and enjoy being out together as a family for the first time in a week. We're here at Disney World, The Magic Kingdom."

I tried to heed her advice and just enjoy myself. I really did. But then it all went south. This was the moment where any smart man, a man who knows his wife, lets go of a bad idea and moves on. (I was obviously not that man at that moment.)

"I'm aware of how hard we've worked to get here," I said, "but you have no idea how difficult it may be to find a dealership that will take care of this problem in a matter of hours."

Connie's tone changed ever so slightly as she replied, "David, I'm asking you to let this go for now. We've come all the way to Orlando, and today is the first day we've made it to the park."

I pushed it a bit further. "I know all this, Connie. What I'm trying to get you to see is that I'm going to be driving twelve hours home with wind pounding in my face unless I get something done with that SUV."

By this point, I had exhausted all of her patience. She spun around with fire in her eyes. "Let it go! Do you hear me? Let it go. You are not leaving this place. You are going to enjoy being with *your* children for a few hours, and we will figure out what to do with the broken window when we leave. Do *not* bring this up with me again!"

We boarded the monorail. I sat down by a small Asian gentleman in his forties, who was wearing a Mickey Mouse T-shirt and a Pluto visor with dangling ears. He looked as ridiculous as I felt at that moment. He, too, had traveled across the universe to get his children to Disney World. We were among the thousands who came there annually, fighting with our spouses, wrangling sick, exhausted, fussy kids all the way to the golden gates, for the opportunity to spend hundreds of dollars for some good, old-fashioned Walt Disney entertainment. I sighed as the door closed, the Disney soundtrack began, and we were off.

"It's a small world after all, it's a small world after all. It's a small world after all, it's a small, small world. . . . It's a world of laughter, a world of cheer . . ."

Later that day, after we had maxed out all three of our sick children, I located a Ford dealership to have them replace the window for the trip home. When I arrived at the dealership, they told me there was no loaner available, and my only option was to wait while they took a look at things. So I camped out in the smoky lounge. The woman next to me was watching a rerun of *The Tyra Banks Show*. It was the episode where Tyra goes undercover as an overweight woman to denounce our prejudices toward fat people.

"You seen this one?" she asked.

"No, I don't really follow Tyra," I remarked.

"Well, just hang on, because none of these men know they are on a date with a supermodel underneath that fat suit. They'll videotape 'em, and then she'll have them boys on the show later and make 'em look like idiots."

"It isn't all that hard to make a man look like an idiot, is it?" I asked my new friend.

"Ain't that the truth."

An hour and a half later, I tried to get a cup of coffee. Cheryl Ann, the parts and service receptionist, informed me that the coffeemaker was broken. Instead, I had Fritos and a Diet Coke out of the snack machine for dinner. As I dropped my coins in the slot, I thought, *If only I owned a Land Rover, someone would be bringing me a cup of Starbucks to drink while they pulled around a 2007 Discovery for me to drive while they addressed my inconvenience.*

Not so for those of us who own a Ford. For us, it's Fritos, Diet Coke, and Tyra Banks—and the only coffee available is the ground beans in the back of my brand new Expedition.

FASTER THAN A SPEEDING BULLET, MORE POWERFUL THAN A LOCOMOTIVE

As I think back on that week in Orlando—the trips to the doctor, the prescriptions, the banana split, the coffee beans, the sleepless nights, the window crashing into the door frame, the monorail, Tyra in her fat suit, and World War III with my wife—I wonder, *What drove me to push so hard to get out for ice cream and then turn around and drag three sick kids to Disney World?* I believe it's the same force that couldn't let up when my wife said, "Let it go." And heck, it's the same thing that moved my father-in-law to start passing his jacket back to Fort Vomit.

We men get so focused on *finding solutions* that we apply it to every situation, including our relationships. And we believe that the answer is mysteriously hidden in some kind of *action*. We are wired for action. Elementally, it points back to the Curse. When something goes haywire in our relationships, it exposes our fear of not being enough, of not having what it takes. We know in our hearts that we're built for war, but we have also experienced the shame of being relationally and emotionally incompetent. We're scared, confused, and powerless, and we may feel ill equipped and unprepared to fix the problem. But that doesn't keep us from trying. We don't trust that our presence is enough. Why would we? It has seldom been enough before. In every other area of our lives, we are expected to *do* something. But here there is nothing we can do to fix it and make it right. For many men, work is where they feel most competent, safe, and productive. At work they keep score; they produce and accomplish. They get rewards.

It works the other way too. A woman doesn't get it when her husband drops the ball at work and is reprimanded and loses a big account. She says something like, "I'm sure there will be another opportunity." She wants to be encouraging and understanding, but her husband looks at her like, "I hate you!" She doesn't comprehend why her compassion doesn't encourage him. It's because she's rarely known what it is to feel impotent.

This manly desire to fix things is played out in the film *White Men Can't Jump.* In the movie, we get a glimpse of the differences between the way men relate to each other and the way they relate to women. The physical sparring on the basketball court is matched by the verbal sparring between the sexes. In one scene, Billy (Woody Harrelson) is hashing it out with Gloria (Rosie Perez). Gloria spends hours hiding out in a hotel room, reading dozens of magazines, filling her head with random information in preparation for the day she gets a shot on *Jeopardy!* One morning, while the couple is lying in bed, they have the following conversation:

Gloria: Honey? My mouth is dry. Honey, I'm thirsty.

Billy: Umm . . . [water runs as he begins to fill a glass]. There you go, honey.

Gloria: When I said I was thirsty, it doesn't mean I want a glass of water.

Billy: It doesn't?

Gloria: You're missing the whole point of me saying I'm thirsty. If I have a problem, you're not supposed to solve it. Men always make the mistake of thinking they can solve a woman's problem. It makes them feel omnipotent.

Billy: Omnipotent? Did you have a bad dream?

Gloria: It's a way of controlling a woman.

Billy: Bringing them a glass of water?

Gloria: Yes. I read it in a magazine. See, if I'm thirsty, I don't want a glass of water. I want you to sympathize. I want you to say, "Gloria, I, too, know what it feels like to be thirsty. I, too, have had a dry mouth." I want you to connect with me through sharing and understanding the concept of dry mouthedness.

Billy: This is all in the same magazine?

Gloria: You're into control.

Billy: Shut up.

Gloria: See?

Billy: You make me sick. [He rolls over in bed and turns his back to her.]

Gloria: Don't give me the rollover.

Billy: When I say I'm thirsty, it means if anybody has a glass of water, I'd love a sip.

Gloria: Exactly the kind of thing I thought you'd say!

In 1966, Michael Lewis, a developmental psychologist, researched sex differences using one-year-olds. Lewis and his colleagues set up a barrier between a child and its mother. The barrier created physical separation, but the child was able to see the mother. Most of the boys attempted to tear down the barrier, whereas most girls stood and wept. Lewis remarked, "The boy child wants to get back to Mom, and it's going to climb over that barrier. It's going to knock it down. It's gonna push on it. It's gonna try to go around the side." It's like Superman to the rescue.

What's interesting to note is that the girls managed to find their way out from behind the barrier faster than their male counterparts. Their strategy came in soliciting help from another person. When the girls showed distress, their mothers emerged from behind the barrier and picked them up. Again, it's all about relationship when it comes to women. And not just about being *in* relationship, but being *heard* and *understood* in relationship. Women are more process oriented than men.

SO WHY CAN'T WE JUST GET ALONG?

For a decade after I (Stephen) graduated from college, I coached highly competitive youth soccer. During that time, I worked closely with boys and girls ranging in age from nine to twenty-one. My first team was a group of ten-year-old girls whom I coached for six years. Initially, I coached these girls like I had been coached—like boys. Looking back at those early seasons, many of those practices were more like boot camp than an atmosphere to develop players.

A few seasons into it, I read the book *Catch Them Being Good,* by then-U.S. Women's National Team coach Tony DiCicco, in which he lays out his approach to coaching women and how it is different from coaching men.[8] A central premise of the book is that girls play for the team, whereas boys play for the glory. As I began to apply the principles of this book to my team, the girls began to flourish. Our times together on and off the field were more centered around relationship, working together, and playing together than they were around learning the game of soccer. The team began to win.

Contrast this experience with the last team I coached, a group of nine-year-old boys. At times, these guys were more interested in competing against one another than in playing an opponent. In practices and in games, they would keep track of how many goals they had scored and compare themselves to each other. I began to see that, even as boys, men are more individualistic, whereas women are more collaborative.

Women have an innate understanding of filling and multiplying. Men have an innate understanding of subduing and ruling. By design, women are process oriented. Men are action oriented. Women create, adorn, beautify, embellish, and decorate. Men shape, move, build, structure, and implement. Women soothe the savage beast. Men slay it. Women nurture and grow. Men erect systems and structures.

The pain of the Curse keeps couples from being willing to

reveal the nature of their souls to each other. When couples try to avoid how hard life is or blame each other for the difficulty, their relationship dies. The woman ends up feeling more alone, and the man ends up feeling like more of a failure. Frequently, a woman will go someplace where she doesn't feel as alone. (More often than not, she'll turn to the kids.) A man will go someplace where he doesn't feel as impotent. (Usually, he will bury himself in his job.) We run from the difficulty of relationship and dependence into the isolation of our own need for control.

In our relationships with the opposite sex, we tend to choose partners who will enable us to hide. At some level, we always choose a mate who we think won't make us change. We pick a person who likes us the way we are and will require the least amount of growth or maturity from us. Women run from their loneliness by finding a man who they think will make them happy. Men run from their sense of failure and futility by finding a woman who they think will respect them. In this way, we avoid our sexuality by choosing a person who we think will help us escape the Curse.

But change is inevitable. Maintaining the status quo takes greater and greater energy. A commitment not to change will kill a relationship, because fighting for homeostasis ends up sucking the life out of the very thing we are trying to protect. How God made us is quite funny if you stop and think about it. There are two parts of the body that we can see only by reflection. One is our face. We need someone else to describe it for us—to tell us we're beautiful. The other part is our backside. We need someone else to tell us when we are being a butt. We can't change without input from an "other." And no one is more "other" than a member of the opposite sex.

Being known by a woman is the place where a man is more vulnerable than any other place in his life. It is where he can most be seen for who he really is—and who he is not. For a woman, the converse is true—she is most a woman when she is comprehended by a man. Opposites not only attract, they provide the opportunity to compare and contrast God's creativity.

Men are more oriented toward focus. Women are more diverse in their perspective. Because their eyes are naturally on the big picture, they're more gifted at complexity. Men, on the other hand, are masters of specificity. Earlier in this chapter, we talked about how brain chemistry differences in women and men give them different approaches to problem solving. Couple that with the spiritual leaning toward filling (women) and building (men), and you have the groundwork for all sorts of conflict and misunderstanding, but also a powerful framework for synergy. A man's core competency leans toward functionality. A woman's is more aesthetic. When living out her gender, a woman's heart is bent to inclusion. Her window to the world is relationship. When a man is most manly, he is more decisive and confident. It's a symphony of might and mercy.

Tenderness without strength (and strength without tenderness) is a perversion of what God intended. Without both qualities in operation, there will always be an incomplete picture.

SO, WHAT'S A WOMAN TO DO?

1. Don't lose sight of how your man is hardwired. Remember Michael Lewis's study of one-year-olds: Most of the boys tried

to tear down the barrier. Men are wired for action right from the start.

2. Think of the effects of the Curse. When something goes haywire in a relationship, it exposes a man's fear of not being enough, of not having what it takes.

3. Ladies, it's okay to remind your man that you are not a problem to be solved but a mystery to be enjoyed.

"YOU'RE TOO SENSITIVE!"

ARE MEN JUST EMOTIONALLY CONSTIPATED?

MY WIFE AND I (Stephen) started dating almost fifteen years ago. Over the course of our relationship, one argument we've had far too often has to do with my inability to balance home and work. Early in our marriage, my workaholic impulses cost us as a couple. Sadly, it wasn't uncommon for me to become absorbed in my work. At times, I became so engrossed in my job that I virtually deserted my wife and kids. Although my tendency to put my job first has not been totally exorcized from our relationship, it has improved as Heather and I have matured and learned how to better resolve conflict. But when we were newlyweds, we sometimes handled our disagreements like Nick Lachey and Jessica Simpson on MTV's reality show *Newlyweds: Nick and Jessica*.

At some point during our second year of marriage, I came

home from work around seven o'clock after pledging earlier in the day that I would be home at five-thirty. When I entered our small, one-bedroom apartment, Heather was on the couch watching TV. I kissed her on the forehead and put down my bag.

"How was your day?" I asked, acting as if nothing were out of the ordinary. Heather didn't respond. She continued to sit calmly, watching a sitcom.

Maybe she didn't hear me, I thought.

I saw that my dinner was on the table—a thick paste of cold spaghetti and sauce that had obviously been sitting there for a while.

No, she heard me.

I guessed that Heather's mood was as cold as my dinner. Still, I hoped for a moment that I could dodge the inevitable argument. I tried again, "Thanks for making dinner. It looks good."

Still no reply.

Then, at a second glance, I noticed that she was not so much watching TV as she was just looking in the direction of the television, faintly grinning. I began to smell the tension, more pungent than the cold pasta and marinara. But, intrepid soul that I am, I decided to make one more attempt at pretending things were okay.

"Hey," I tossed out casually, "I'm sorry I'm late again. I know how important it is to you that I come home on time. But I got caught up working on a project and lost track of time." Then I sat down to dinner.

(Okay, I know what you're thinking: *what a stupid, insensitive, self-absorbed jerk.* You're right. I was.)

Heather had not even acknowledged my presence. Not a

blink. Not a nod. Not a shrug. But as I sat down to eat my cold pasta, she slowly, calmly, and deliberately turned and rose from the sofa. She stood motionless and expressionless, looking at me for what must have been thirty seconds—just long enough to make me really afraid but not long enough for me to break the silence. Then she began to speak.

I don't remember what she said or how I replied, except that after a few sentences the conversation escalated into a full-blown war: name-calling, threatening, cussing, shaming, and then silence. The room was knee-deep with contempt, disappointment, and doubt. It ended with Heather grabbing her car keys, running out of the apartment, and speeding off.

Some time later, she called from a pay phone to let me know she was safe. I tried to apologize, but it somehow morphed into blaming her for overreacting, and we plummeted right back into conflict. In her rage, Heather violently hung up the phone. Another several hours passed before she came home, and it took several more hours of working through it before we finally made up.

Once we'd reconciled, she led me out to the car and pointed to the driver's side mirror. It dangled from the door by a thin cable, like a severed appendage on an injured soldier. Apparently, after she hung up on me, she sped away but ripped off the mirror on the pay phone. Thankfully, our relationship recovered, and the mirror was the most severe damage from the day.

In our struggles to learn how to manage conflict, Heather and I are not alone. Wherever humans are involved in relationship, conflict is unavoidable. This is especially true when it comes to women and men.

There are generally three types of couples: those who fight fairly, those who fight dirty, and those who are stuck in denial, insisting "We never fight at all." Conflict is inevitable. It's not a question of whether or not you will disagree; what really matters is what you do with the conflict when it comes along.

NO ONE'S IMMUNE

In order to get a clear picture of conflict between the sexes, we have to look through the lens of marriage, because most of the research about how women and men argue has been done within the context of marriage. But even if you're single, you're not off the hook; this still applies to you.

Most people are aware that the national divorce rate is somewhere around 40 or 50 percent for first marriages.[1] (That number almost doubles for second and third marriages.)[2] And though the incidence of divorce has been on a gradual decline for several years, the number of couples that cohabitate has increased tenfold during the last few decades.[3] (These relationships are overwhelmingly short-term.) Because shacking up has lost its stigma, more and more people are choosing to forgo the commitment of marriage and opt for living together. Even when people decide to get married, it's not for long. Twenty-five percent of all first marriages last less than a decade.[4] One in two divorces occurs within the first seven years of marriage.[5]

What is at the root of all this relational failure? Many divorces occur partly because couples are not ready for marriage—they are uneducated, immature, and unprepared. Engaged couples usually spend far more time preparing for the wedding ceremony than for their marriage relationships. The average cost of a wedding in the United States is more than twenty thousand dollars.[6] In contrast, ten premarital counseling sessions with a licensed marriage counselor cost approximately $900–$1,500 (depending on where you live). A second significant reason many more couples don't make it is because they don't know how to use conflict to enhance their relationships. What's going on?

Have you ever wondered how two people who love each other so much can hate each other so vehemently? Well, for one thing, love and hate aren't opposites. The opposite of love and hate is *apathy*. Love and hate can frequently co-occur in relationships—especially when it comes to men and women. This ambivalence is often at the heart of conflict. What we do with this tension will determine whether we learn and grow from conflict or become hard-hearted, resentful, or apathetic.

By looking at conflict from three perspectives (relational, biological, and spiritual), we can gain a better understanding of its roots and how we can use conflict for the benefit of our relationships instead of to their detriment.

THE DANCE OF CONFLICT

What do couples argue about the most? Money and children, in that order. But there's a whole lot of research that tells us it's not necessarily what couples argue about but rather *how* they argue that predicts dissatisfaction.[7] The most common hurdles for men and women in conflict are negative styles of relating with each other—arguments that rapidly become negative, putdowns, sarcasm, overlooking the positive in the relationship, and the dreaded silent treatment.

Relationship researcher Dr. John Gottman has spent three

decades researching what makes marriages succeed or fail. As one of America's leading marital experts, Gottman's research has enabled him to predict with greater than 90 percent accuracy if a marriage will end in divorce. The crux of his research looks at how mismanaged conflict and negative interactions in marriage predict divorce.

Dr. Gottman's numerous studies have identified at least four distinct practices—which he candidly describes as "The Four Horsemen of the Apocalypse"—that are like nails in the coffin of a relationship:

- Criticism (complaining)
- Defensiveness
- Stonewalling
- Contempt[8]

Couples who avoid these negative tactics during conflict have greater intimacy, trust, and relational longevity. They are able to maintain successful relationships.

When it comes to conflict in male-female relationships, it often feels more like mosh pit slam-dancing than an elegant waltz or a passionate tango. But when men and women disagree, there is a pretty consistent pattern of interaction. It goes something like this:

1. The woman is usually the one who brings up "issues."
2. She usually also presents an analysis of the problem.
3. She may also suggest solutions to the problem.

This is the positive side. However, at the same time that a woman names the issue, offers insight, and suggests solutions,

1. She's likely to do it really hastily, before the man can even get on the same page.
2. Being flustered, the man stonewalls, stalls, and doesn't respond.
3. Feeling rejected, the woman grows defensive and demanding.
4. When she demands, what does he do? He withdraws.[9]

This is a grueling and abusive style of relating. If couples are unable to learn a different communication pattern, they usually end up divorced. While caught in this counterproductive dance, many women have wondered, "Are men just emotionally constipated?" Men, on the other hand, infer that "women are just too sensitive."

Men and women must change the manner in which they engage in conflict—from beginning to end—if they hope to love each other well. Don't be confused here: It's not really a communication problem; it's a heart problem. Most conflict between women and men is not an issue with who said what; it has more to do with the content of their character and the trust they have in each other.

We've all heard of the pop-psychology concept of "active listening" ("So, what I hear you saying is . . ."). But here's something that maybe you haven't heard: It doesn't really work. Despite what many well-intentioned counselors, psychologists, and social workers teach their clients, researchers have proven repeatedly that active listening doesn't help resolve conflict.

According to studies, the most successful long-term

relationships rarely use techniques such as paraphrasing or summarizing each other's statements. These couples also almost never "validate" each other's feelings.[10] Instead, what these couples have in common is a level of trust and commitment that does not waver during conflict. Conflict for the most successful couples rarely degenerates into tearing each other apart or belittling each other. Arguments may become heated, but there are no character attacks or name-calling.

STARTING BEHIND THE EIGHT BALL

Caroline is the kind of woman who, when she enters a room, every eye is immediately drawn to her. She has dark hair, olive skin, and large, deep, expressive eyes. It's not just her physical beauty that guys notice; it's her presence. She's as passionate and charismatic as she is stunningly beautiful. Furthermore, one is immediately drawn into conversation with her. She is brilliant, deeply intuitive, articulate, and highly opinionated on a number of topics and issues.

Phillip is the type of guy who could make other men feel threatened, because women of all ages are immediately drawn to him. It's not unusual, in a large group of mixed company, to see every female eye turn and remain fixated on him. He is classically handsome, with blond hair, blue eyes, and a stop-you-in-your-tracks smile. In addition to his looks, he is adventurous, somewhat mysterious, equally passionate, deeply curious, and considered hopelessly charming by every woman he encounters.

Caroline and Phillip have an incredible connection with each other. It is both fascinating to watch and mind-boggling to experience. Although they've known each other for only thirteen months, it's as if they've been together for fifty-plus years. They have that kind of relationship where one of them begins a sentence and the other is magically able to finish it without a pause. They are *that* in tune with each other. You know the type: a couple that seems more like siblings than companions.

It had been several weeks since I (David) had last seen either Caroline or Phillip, until we were together recently. It was a large group, and we had been engaged in conversation for only a short time, but I was immediately reminded of how much I enjoy their company and the lively dialogue that always emerges.

When Phillip saw Caroline for the first time on this particular day, he began chanting, "Candy, Candy!"

Caroline looked at him with disgust and remarked, "Phillip, my name is Caroline, so don't call me Candy!"

Phillip only increased the passion and volume of his words. "Candy, Candy!"

Caroline responded with more energy behind her words: "Stop saying my name that way. I don't know what you're talking about. I told you, Phillip, my name is not Candy. Candy is what you get at a birthday party or when you put poo poo in the potty." (Have I mentioned that Caroline and Phillip are both two years old?)

Candy—I mean, Caroline—paused for a quarter of a second to catch her breath and then launched out again. "Mr. David, do you know why he calls me that? He thinks my name is Candy, and I think he's so silly."

By this point in their conversation, she had knocked a bit of the wind out of Phillip's sails, but he continued with the interaction. "Candy," he said with less vigor but while looking at her face with longing and affection.

"I'm putting on my lipstick, Phillip, and I'm not looking at you," she said. (Keep in mind she's two.)

Phillip stared at her with confusion as she applied Chap-Stick to her chin and ears. Then he emerged with renewed passion in what appeared to be a last-ditch effort. "Candy, Candy!"

Caroline completely ignored him this time as she continued with her cosmetics.

THE GRUNT AND THE GURGLE

Even though they are only two, Phillip and Caroline are surprisingly similar to a number of adult couples we see in our counseling practices. The man does his share of grunting and staring with confusion, while his wife, fiancée, or girlfriend speaks her mind. The interchange between the couple is playful, chock-full of energy, ripe with the opportunity for conflict, oftentimes dangerously predictable, and occasionally teetering perilously on the edge of failure.

But if we see these same differences between the sexes in children as young as two, when does it all begin? How do we become creatures who act, speak, think, and respond so differently?

Anne Moir and David Jessel, in their book *Brain Sex,* describe how newborn girls, even when they are only a few hours old, are more sensitive to touch than boys. Research involving finger and hand sensitivity produced "differences so striking that sometimes male and female scores do not even overlap, the most sensitive boy feeling less than the least sensitive girl."[11] These findings suggest that other senses may also be more acute. According to Moir and Jessel, "Baby girls become irritated and anxious about noise, pain, or discomfort more readily than baby boys."[12] So, apparently right out of the chute, women really are more sensitive than men.

And this sensitivity doesn't end with the five physical senses. From the earliest moments of life, and before they can even understand language, girls appear to be better at identifying and experiencing the emotional content of speech. For example, infant girls are more easily soothed by singing and hearing comforting words. From the outset of life, infant girls demonstrate a stronger interest in communication with other people.

In a study of two- to four-day-old infants, the girls stared for a longer period of time at a speaking adult and twice as long as boys at a silent adult making eye contact. The same study identified that girls were more likely to gurgle at other people. The boys were found to be just as talkative but content to jabber and grunt at toys and abstract geometric objects. This bias emerged again when at four months of age girls could distinguish between photographs of familiar people and strangers, whereas boys could not.[13]

Fast-forward a few decades, and here is what this difference sounds like between a wife and husband.

Wife: "Hey, honey, how was your day?"

Husband: "Fine."

Wife: "Didn't you present to the board today?"

Husband: "Yeah."

Wife: "And it went okay?"

Husband: "Sure."

Wife: "And how is Edward? I heard he and Sheila are expecting?"

Husband: "They're fine."

Wife: "Well, that's great. I know they'll be wonderful parents. I should pick up something for them this weekend, shouldn't I?"

Husband: "Yeah."

DIFFERENT RULES, SAME GAME

In many couples' experiences, the preceding interaction is only slightly exaggerated, if at all. Gender differences are woven in and out of everyday conversations. We can't lump all women and men into programmed categories, but the ridiculous misinterpretations that plague female/male conversations can be explained by the different rules of conversation by which men and women play. For example, researchers have identified that men tend to be more direct in their communication and use fewer words in their interactions.[14]

The differences don't stop there. Male and female adult conversation patterns can be traced back to the ways in which boys and girls interact on the grade school playground. Girls often choose interactions in a small group where they sit and talk with one another. Boys, on the other hand, tend to choose larger group contexts that involve a task or an activity.[15] Girls utilize language and conversation for the purpose of establishing and maintaining relationship connections. Boys, on the other hand, see conversation as a means of exchanging information and negotiating terms or status. It's no wonder that the little exchange between Caroline and Phillip was so typical of conversations between men and women. The patterns of communication have been established and reinforced by nature *and* nurture for our entire lives.

BOYS AND GIRLS

The dance between men and women looks more like a tango than a waltz—more an "interaction marked by a lack of straightforwardness" than an exchange that "advances easily and successfully."[16]

One important factor in cross-gender communication is the way in which boys and girls differ. For example, compared to little girls, many boys are emotionally illiterate. Boys don't have the same ability as girls to articulate their emotions or read the emotions of others. Boys feel and sense things as strongly as their female counterparts, but they just don't know what to do with their emotions or how to express what stirs in their hearts.

By the age of nine or ten, boys will begin to express primary feelings (such as fear, sadness, guilt, and hurt) as anger. They talk less about what they're feeling, and they cry far less than girls. There is a greater tendency to hide in their rooms, kick, yell, pick fights, or brood. Boys often experience confusion about the sadness, fear, and loneliness they feel. Anger and aggression are considered to be culturally acceptable for boys, even masculine defining. There are few role models for boys as to what emotions look like in a man's life.

Many a mother has had a conversation like this with her son when he comes home from school:

Mom: "Hey, honey. How was school today?"

123

Son: "Fine."

Mom: "Anything exciting or different happening at school?"

Son: "No."

Mom: "I heard there is a dance after the game this Friday night."

Son: "Yeah."

Mom: "Are you planning to go?"

Son: "Maybe."

Mom: "Well, how are your friends?"

Son: "Fine."

Mom: "Any tests coming up?"

Son: "What is this, twenty questions? I said everything is fine!"

The difference between girls and boys carries right on in to adulthood. One area that reveals how differently men and women handle emotions is the realm of conflict. We believe that men and women both share a tendency to avoid conflict, but they do it for different reasons. Men avoid conflict because they thrive on resolution for the sake of *consolidation*. Men function as if life is a problem waiting to be solved and they're just the guy for the job. Therefore, men will engage in conflict when they see it as an opportunity for solution. Life, work, and relationships are viewed as a series of conquests, a puzzle to be mastered, a loose end to tie up, or a game to win (or to at least emerge from as the high scorer).

In certain contexts, men will engage in conflict as an opportunity to compete. Men are pack animals, and when they get together, one will always emerge as the alpha dog. Sit in the corner of any boardroom or office and watch the men at play with one another. The business world is like one giant football field when it comes to men, and all of life can be viewed as a contest.

Male conversations tend to rely heavily on competition and establishing dominance. Men see themselves as individuals in a hierarchical social order. Furthermore, men—intentionally or not—tend to negotiate while engaged in conversations, as a means of maintaining status and position. Don't believe this to be true? Find your way to any youth baseball field, soccer match, or basketball court on any given Saturday morning. The athletes don't have to be any older than four years old for this phenomenon to be played out. Watch the dads. Listen to what they say. (This is actually a setting where men *really* talk.)

While coaching our daughters' soccer team when the girls were four, we actually had a dad light into us about our choice not to reschedule a game that was canceled due to rain. He actually said, "We came out here to play, man, not to have fun." Our response was something along the lines of, "Man, these girls are here for the matching green uniforms and the gummy snacks after the game. Let's get real."

Women avoid conflict because they thrive on resolution for the sake of *restoration*. Because relationships tend to be at the center of a woman's existence, they experience disequilibrium when there is tension in their relationships. Women will engage in conflict when they see an opportunity for restoration and reconciliation. They aren't afraid to enter the fray if they believe the outcome may guarantee a deeper relationship, connection, or mutual understanding.

I (David) experienced this phenomenon recently while on a date with my five-year-old daughter. Our date night included dinner and a trip to the theater. At my daughter's request, we dined on gourmet peanut butter and jelly sandwiches, affectionately known as the Ooey-Gooey Special at one of our favorite neighborhood eateries. Following dinner, we went to see a production of *Cinderella*.

At the theater, she and I sat side by side, watching the pumpkin transform into a carriage, the mice evolve into white horses, and the handmaiden magically become the object of the prince's affection. The classic story played out in all its glory and wonder. As we reached the arc of the story, the shoe was brought to the house and tried on by the evil stepsisters, and of course it didn't fit. The herald then asked, "Are there any other women residing in this house?" The evil stepmother answered harshly, "No," and the herald prepared to leave.

At this moment of crisis, my daughter squeezed my hand with a look of distress on her face. I leaned into her and whispered, "Oh, no. He doesn't know that Cinderella has been locked in the attic." My daughter squeezed my hand tighter. As I looked at her gentle eyes full of distress and hope, I was reminded that a female never experiences the weight of conflict quite as intensely as she does when it resides at the center of a relationship.

If Cinderella never had the opportunity to try on the glass slipper, the prince would never know that she was the poor hand-maiden he had danced with at the ball. It was Cinderella who captured his heart with her beauty and her presence. But she was trapped in the attic as the opportunity for true love disintegrated two stories below.

The only peace my daughter experienced at that moment came from her familiarity with the story. (She has seen the Disney movie and read the story only a few hundred times.) As she beckoned her mind back to the inevitable resolution, she yelled out to me and everyone seated around us, "Don't worry, Dad, the mice will let her out of the attic. *She will try on the glass slipper!*" We all began to chuckle as she stared at the stage with great hope and anticipation. She could handle the conflict of the story as long as restoration of the relationship was on the horizon. Once the poor maiden ended up in the arms of the prince, balance was restored to the universe.

"RE-SOLVING" CONFLICT

There is a way of resolving conflict in a relationship that can actually build intimacy and trust. It's not a matter of figuring out how not to fight; it's a matter of figuring out how to fight well. Many, many couples fight for all the wrong reasons. If we are to fight well in our relationships, we have to reevaluate the basis of our arguments. As we look to resolve conflict in marriage, we need to find new solutions. We need to learn how to "re-solve" our conflicts. Re-solving conflict is a new way of looking at conflict, a way in which arguing can become one of the most intimate, fulfilling, and affirming parts of our relationships. (We know that sounds contradictory, but hang with us for another minute or two, and it will all come into focus.)

The first principle of "re-solving" conflict is recognizing that men and women are made for drama. Life is full of tension. Conflict is everywhere. At our very deepest spiritual level, we are made for excitement, we long for passion, and we are attracted to drama. We are people who love stories. Stories permeate our lives. We are drawn to them. We live in them. We crave them. Whether it's movies, television, books, theme parks, theater, opera, music, history, family reunions, or whatever, stories are at the heart of our lives. You could say that we're story people. An essential part of every story is conflict. To "re-solve" conflict, we need to stop avoiding tension and learn to appreciate conflict for what it is—the rush of life and the prelude to resolution. How do we avoid tension?

The Bible especially reflects the significance of story. One big reason why the ancient texts remain relevant to us today is that they are primarily narrative. Sometimes referred to as "the greatest story ever told," the Bible is full of stories. The passages in Scripture that teach us most about God and about ourselves are largely story based. So, like us, God must love stories. And, if he loves stories, he has to love drama, conflict, and tension. Without tension, drama, and conflict, there could be no hope, no transformation, and no redemption—no resolution. In the Bible, as with our lives, tension is inescapable, disagreement likely, and drama everywhere.

As story people, our relationships, by their nature, are replete with trouble—two people, so different, trying to navigate life together. The fullest expression of relationship between a man and a woman is marriage. With its potential for conflict, marriage is God's primary playground for making men and women more like him. This leads us to the second principle of "re-solving" conflict: Conflict brings with it the possibility of transformation and growth. Are we open to change?

Conflict is threatening. It feels dangerous because it exposes our deepest needs and desires, without promising resolution. Whenever we enter conflict, we are vulnerable to being abandoned, harmed, or disappointed. This is the third principle of "re-solving" conflict: Conflict exposes our heart and draws us to be present. Will you tell the truth about me?

Marriage-and-family-therapy pioneer Virginia Satir writes, "I believe the greatest gift I can conceive of having from anyone is to be seen, heard, understood, and touched by them. The greatest gift I can give is to see, hear, understand, and touch another person. When this is done, I feel contact has been made."[17] Satir wasn't talking about conflict, but she might as well have been. When we enter conflict without defensiveness, we have the opportunity for our deepest needs and desires to deeply touch another person.

The Bible says it a bit differently: "A man will leave his father and mother and be united to his wife, and they will become one flesh."[18] Both Virginia Satir and the writer of Genesis get at the same point: To be known by and to fully know another person is what life is all about. Conflict can get in the way of relationship, but it doesn't have to. This is the final principle of "re-solving" conflict: Conflict leads to intimacy, passion, and compassion. Will I engage the other?

BARRIERS TO "RE-SOLVING" CONFLICT

What is the problem in any relationship if it's not conflict? What keeps us from entering the tension of conflict with the hope for transformation and intimacy? What keeps us from "making contact" with each other? What keeps us from being passionate and compassionate with each other? The number one barrier to "re-solving" conflict is how we cope with heartache.

We've all experienced moments of conflict in life that have brought us heartache without resolution. Whether it was our parents' divorce, the death of a loved one, the ending of a significant relationship, someone harming or violating us, or being made fun of, everyone is a casualty of some sort of painful heartache. We all bear the marks of wounded hearts. We've all been betrayed and felt powerless. We've learned ways to cope with our desire for relationship without having to expose our hearts. We've found ways to get our needs met without being vulnerable to pain.

In these ways, women and men are more alike than different. Despite our differences, we have some pretty striking similarities. We all long to be known, accepted, and loved by another. At the end of the day, men and women want the same things. We all long for relationships marked with intimacy, authenticity, and pleasure, but conflict disrupts all this. Conflict shows our cards. It reveals what we are passionate about and desire most deeply. Conflict occurs when what I want and what you want are different.

In order for our relationships to have intimacy and authenticity during conflict, we must ask ourselves two questions:

1. Is God good?
2. Are we (as a couple) *for* each other?

To the degree that we avoid wrestling with these questions in our daily lives, we cannot have intimacy with God. If we lack intimacy with God, we will always lack true intimacy with other people—especially with the opposite sex, and especially during conflict. How we answer these two questions directly affects how well we will fight.

The question of God's goodness may express itself in a number of ways: "God, do you care?" "God, do you meet needs?" "God, do you see me?" "God, do you delight in me?" We can never address other people in conflict until we have resolved the issue of whether we truly trust God's goodness. At points in our lives we ask, "God, how can I trust you when you say you love me but you won't keep me from pain?" If we don't really trust God, we cannot rest in the fact that he has provided our spouses to us as a means of making us more into the people he wants us to be. Trusting God means that we can begin to look at our spouses as God's provision for our holiness.

Before we can "re-solve" conflict well, we must resolve to be *for* the other person. When we look across the table at the person with whom we are fighting, can we honestly say that we're in this together? This primary question leads naturally to several others:

1. Does he or she tell me the truth? Do I tell him or her the truth?
2. Is he or she willing to stand in my way (if necessary)? Am I willing to stand in his or her way (if necessary)?

3. Will he or she invest in my pleasure? Do I invest in his or her pleasure? (In other words, are we concerned about and committed to each other's happiness?)
4. Is he or she grateful for me? Am I grateful for him or her?
5. Does he or she delight in my presence? Do I delight in his or her presence?

Until we can honestly say that *yes,* God is good and we trust him, and *yes,* we are *for* the other person in the relationship, there is little hope that our conflicts will end in anything more than a pact to agree to disagree or a negotiated compromise that is something less than win-win. No one is really changed in the process. No one matures. The peace may be kept, but wounds aren't healed—and God is not glorified.

However, when we can answer yes to these two questions, it will change the way we engage in conflict. Instead of fighting to be right or to prove a point, we will begin to fight on behalf of the ones we love. We fight with their best interests at heart. We fight for their higher good. We fight for their dignity. No longer will we fight to be safe or to get our way; instead, we will enter conflict with a heart for something much more beautiful: for God's glory to be revealed in the life of the other person.

SO, WHAT'S A WOMAN TO DO?

1. Give some thought to how you saw conflict handled, or not handled, when you were growing up. Consider how your past experience influences your present relationships when it comes to conflict.

2. Keep in mind that *fighting well* can become a means of building intimacy.

3. Ask yourself the five questions at the end of this chapter and see what comes from your responses.

4. The next time you are in an argument with your man, picture him naked. You'll get a good laugh.

8
"WHAT WERE YOU THINKING?"

I (DAVID) RECENTLY had a conversation with a good friend who shared a story with me about her husband . . . her husband and a mouse. One evening, when her kids were about two and eight, she was relaxing in the den watching television when she saw a mouse run across the floor. She hates mice. Somewhat frantically, she asked her husband to set a trap and vowed that she would stay out of the room indefinitely, until the mouse was confirmed dead. With a gleam in his eye, her husband said he had a much better idea. She remembers thinking, *"This is never a good sign."*

His idea involved catching the mouse unharmed, so that he could show it to the kids and then release it back to the wild. He thought this would be a wonderful educational experience for their two-year-old and a wild adventure (à la *Animal Planet*) for their eight-year-old son.

The first attempt to catch the mouse unharmed caused it to scamper up into the lining of one of the den chairs. Undaunted, her husband disappeared briefly and returned with his daughter's plastic play pool and a can of WD-40. At this point, she remembers thinking, *"You're kidding, right?"*

His idea was to spray the inside of the pool with the WD-40 and then place the whole armchair into the pool. He would bring the whole contraption outside and give it a good shake, thus causing the mouse to fall out of the underside of the chair and into the pool. The mouse could not possibly scamper because of the WD-40. This made perfect sense to him. This, of course, made absolutely no sense to her at all.

It wasn't until the chair was in the greased pool that he realized there would be no way to get the chair and the pool through the door to the outside. So he decided to shake the chair inside, which he did. And, lo and behold, the mouse fell out into the pool and could not, in fact, get out due to his greasy little paws. Success!

The next step was to catch the mouse with a piece of Tupperware so that Daddy could show it to the kids before ceremoniously releasing the mouse into the wild to return to its family . . . a real Disney/Pixar moment. These hopes were unceremoniously dashed, however, when he accidentally slammed the mouse in the head with the Tupperware bowl, killing it instantly. There lay little Stuart Little, motionless and coated in WD-40. As their daughter began sobbing, my friend looked at her husband as if to say, *"What were you thinking?"*

EVEN DUMBER THAN HE LOOKS

In the same genre, my (David's) wife would tell the story of the time I destroyed our son's pacifier. He was three at the time, and we had been lazy in having him give it up. He only used it at night and nap time (and on the rare occasion when we just needed him to pipe down).

Our pediatrician, the dentist, and friends had commented on the pacifier at one time or another. A three-year-old buddy of Baker's said, "Hey, why you got that baby binky in your mouth?" I had visions of my son slipping it out from his pillowcase on Boy Scout campouts once everyone was asleep and waking up to his fellow scouts standing around the campfire chanting, "Your oatmeal's ready, little baby! Can we warm your bottle?" I imagined him climbing into bed on his wedding night and asking his bride not to kiss him on the lips after sex because he needed to put his "special retainer" in.

So, one evening I snuck upstairs and cut the tip off his pacifier. I decided I would give him the old "well, looky there; it was so old it just broke right off" story that we had given his older sister at her weaning. He would grieve the loss, we'd have a night of restless sleep, and then move on from there.

Well, I forgot one important detail. I really did mean to talk with my wife before I did it, but I just forgot. I saw the paci lying on Baker's pillow, cut the tip, and went about my business. Connie came home a few hours later as I was heading out to meet a friend for coffee.

Ten minutes into my conversation at the coffee house, my cell phone rang. It was my wife.

"Hey sweetheart, what's up?" I said cheerfully.

"Your son, THAT'S WHAT'S UP! He is upstairs screaming in his bed, crying out for his paci."

My stomach sank.

"David, what were you *thinking?*"

I didn't have time to answer, because that question was followed by another and another and another.

"Were you thinking *at all* when you did that? Did it cross your mind to discuss it with me first? At any moment, did you stop to consider that *you* would be leaving town and leaving *me* with a crying, screaming toddler who likely won't nap in the day or sleep through the night for countless days?" (I had also managed to forget that I was leaving on a work trip two days later.)

I tried to respond, I really did, but she just kept asking more questions, and each question had this incredible energy behind it.

"And why *now?* Why did you choose *today* of all days? What possessed you to do this on this particular day without having talked with me first?"

Finally, I managed to get a word in edgewise. (And thankfully I've learned a thing or two from watching other men fumble the ball in my office.) I immediately agreed with her. "You're absolutely right, Connie. I should have talked with you first. I'm sorry I didn't consult with you before doing that."

(Now here's where it really went south. If only I had stopped with my simple apology and let her finish unleashing on me, I might have come out okay.)

"But honey," I said, "I don't think there would have ever been a good time to have done this. Admit to me that you would have *never* been *really* ready to go through the battle of him giving it up."

The next thing I knew, we had lost our connection. I looked at my cell phone, but I had a full signal. This told me that my wife had terminated our call. When I attempted to call her back, she didn't answer the phone. Maybe *she* had a bad signal. Yeah, right.

I waited a few minutes and called again. Connie answered the phone with a simple "Yes?" But it wasn't a friendly "yes." Not like, "Yes, my love," or, "Yes, we have chocolate chips on the third shelf of the pantry." It was that other "yes," the non-friendly one. I stumbled around for a moment or two with my words and then just confessed, "I'm an idiot, and I'm so sorry." She agreed with me and forgave me (like four days later).

I had a perfectly good reason for doing what I did. My wife had a perfectly good reason for being furious. Over the life of our marriage, we have discovered that we do this dance with one another. She frequently holds back, I often plow ahead. She approaches decisions cautiously and with much thought and attention. I race into decisions without thinking through the long-term effects. This dance has been the source of much conflict in our marriage. Left up to my wife, my son really might have graduated from high school with his binky hanging from the tassel on his cap. Left to my own devices, I tend to plow people over in the process of getting what I want.

Both stories illustrate how a woman gets to the place of asking, "What the heck is he thinking?" Great question. Her next question may be "Was he thinking at all?" The sum of it all is this: Women have *always* had questions about men. Women *will* always have questions about men. And for that matter, men will always have questions about women. We are complex creatures—complicated, fascinating, mysterious, diverse, and different. Fascinatingly similar and unbelievably different. But even so, we still have to get along.

Men and women generally relate in one of five ways: friends, colleagues, couples, spouses, and relatives. In each of these areas, there are significant interactions between men and women that can either bless or curse their relationships.

FRIENDS

Can women and men be friends? Sure. Not only is it possible, but it is good for us to have the perspective of the opposite sex. However, when someone asks, "Can women and men be friends?" what he or she is usually asking is, "Can women and men interact in such a way that sexuality is not an issue?" The answer is *no!* Because it's who we are (not just a part of who we are), sexuality is always at play. In those relationships where one, or both, of the participants tries to hide and/or ignore gender, someone gets hurt.

All relationships with affinity have momentum toward intimacy. Without responsible boundaries and conventions, any relationship can become oversexualized. Friends who are irresponsible and unaware of their hearts and motivations will use the sexuality of their relationships in illegitimate ways. Relationships between men and women are in the most danger of crossing platonic lines when the participants are not aware of the presence, effect, and power of sexuality in their relationships.

COLLEAGUES

What about at work? Sadly, work is a place where sexuality can get really twisted. I (Stephen) was talking with a successful physician the other day who was recounting her professional setting. She remarked, "It's almost like in order for me to be successful at the hospital I have to strip myself of my femininity."

Can women and men both be doctors? Absolutely, but how they go about their duties might look really different if they each remain loyal to their gender. It's not about competence; it's about style. In the workplace, however, we often try to neuter women and men so that we don't have to deal with the added complexity of sexuality. Or we disparage the other sex, castigating them as "witches" (women) or "wimps" (men).

COUPLES

One common way in which men and women relate is in dating relationships. The dilemma here is that both parties are trying to put their best foot forward and therefore often give a false impression of who they are. Dating is a time when quirks and traits ought to be brought into the open, but more typically it's a time when we lie to each other with good intentions—because otherwise we'd never get married.

Only in the last two thousand years has the notion of romantic love even been central to dating and marriage. Prior to that, in almost every culture, arranged marriages were the norm. (In some cultures, it is still prevalent today.) Back then, you met your spouse more often than not on the day of your wedding. Are we saying that dating is wrong? No. Do we recommend "kissing dating good-bye"? No. What we are suggesting is that most dating is useless if you are trying to find a soul mate, because dating by its nature is disingenuous.

SPOUSES

The role of marriage is to reveal God's glory and help us become more like Jesus. Which is to say, one primary function of marriage is to expose our darkness. If a marriage doesn't expose the sin in our hearts and our lives, then it's not a good marriage.

We hope that the DNA of your marriage is such that your very worst—your sin, your shame, and your pain—can be seen. Why? Because we never let our worst be seen by anyone unless we trust him or her. Have you ever raged at your boss? Not likely. (We might behind their backs, of course, but never to their faces.) Why not? Probably because we don't trust them with our hearts.

Our wives, Connie and Heather, have seen the worst of us more than any other people on the face of the earth. We have harmed them more than anyone else. What a compliment to them—and how tragic at the same time. The very nature of marriage is that if we are going to love well, we will also sin terribly.

RELATIVES

Much like marriage, family is another context in which sexuality plays itself out through gender roles. But unlike marriage, the greater number of cross-gender interactions makes family all the more complex. Whether it's mothers and fathers; fathers and daughters; mothers and sons; or brothers and sisters (not to mention grandparents, aunts and uncles and cousins, or siblings and parents from blended families) sexuality is an ever-present factor.

Nowhere can men and women be so ridiculous as with family. There is no other situation where a forty-year-old CEO can revert to acting like (and being treated like) a child (and have it be okay) than with his doting mother. Where else can an award-winning thirty-five-year-old female writer with a Ph.D. not have anything valuable to say than at the Thanksgiving dinner table with her brothers?

SO, WHAT'S A WOMAN TO DO?

Part of breaking the male code is acknowledging and embracing that men and women were never intended to be identical, or even all that much alike. There are so many rich, complicated opportunities in our differences: opportunities for growth and maturity; opportunities for change and transformation.

In God's infinite wisdom (and, we've got to believe, with his sense of humor), he made us as women and men. When we think of our differences, we will always think of our bodies, but it doesn't stop there. Gender is not just DNA, hormones, and body parts. There is much more substance of character below and beyond all the flesh and bones and biochemistry. Gender is not only about genitalia. Our sexuality runs deeper than that—it permeates our souls.

As God's image bearers, we are relational beings engendered as men or women. This means that our gender is always a factor in our relationships. What it means to be feminine or masculine is physiological for sure, but it's also about character and being. What we hope we have shown you is that God absolutely loves the interplay and tension between men and women. Sexuality is not meant to be superficial. It's meant to reveal God's glory. Sex is never meant to define us; it's just a part of a curious conversation between men and women. Relationships between women and men are both odd and glorious, confounding and clarifying, messy and mysterious.

So, what the heck is he doing?

He's being a man: a big, stupid, brilliant, emotionally constipated, wonderfully complex, slightly arrogant, sex-crazed, courageous, strong, clueless, mind-boggling man. That's what the heck he's doing. Being a man and being all those things that come with the package of masculinity: the good and the bad; the glorious and the grotesque.

And what the heck is she doing?

She's being a woman: a beautiful, deep, wonderfully complex, emotionally layered, relationally driven, slightly critical, courageous, strong, clueless, mind-boggling woman. That's what the heck she's doing. Being a woman and being all the things that come with the package of femininity: the good and the bad; the tender and the treacherous.

Of course, as men and women, we are doing all these things simultaneously. And that's where it gets really crazy.

9
CONCLUSION

AFTER ALL THAT, you expected us to have a conclusion?

INTRODUCTION

BEFORE WE BEGIN

1. What are some reasons you want to read this book?
2. What are you hoping to gain from this book?

GETTING STARTED

1. What was your first date like?
2. What about your first kiss?
3. What was your worst date ever?

CHAPTER 1

1. Take a few minutes to brainstorm and create a top ten list of the most important qualities, characteristics, traits, and attributes of your "ideal/perfect" companion. Be creative and cover all areas of relationship (money, personality, spirituality, sex, family history, etc.)
2. Of the list from question one, what are your top three? Which ones are "must haves"? What are you willing to sacrifice or do without?
3. Men and women can really miss connecting with each other when it comes to conversation. Name a time when you were

frustrated or let down by a man's lack of words or his verbal passivity?

4. Fill in the blanks:

Men tend to be more adept at _____ than women. Women tend to be more adept at _____ than men. (Fill in the blanks with as many words or phrases as you can think of.)

5. If you are involved in a romantic relationship, identify an area of longing, an area you desire to see in your companion that is not present.

6. When it comes to men and women, there is often more being said than what is put into words. Read the following phrases:

a. I don't care; whatever you want to do.
b. Nevermind.
c. I can fix that.
d. Looks like we're getting low on gas.
e. Shouldn't we have been there by now?

- If a woman were saying these things, what might be her underlying motive or meaning?

a. _____
b. _____
c. _____
d. _____
e. _____

- If a man were saying these things, what might be his underlying motive or meaning?

a. _____
b. _____

c. _____

d. _____

e. _____

CHAPTER 2

1. Who do you think invented the GPS navigation system, a man or a woman?
2. If there were hidden cameras in your car's console and high-tech microphone devices in the dashboard, what kind of exchanges would be recorded during a driving trip to someplace unfamiliar?
3. Who drives the car most often in your relationship, the man or the woman? Why? What might happen if on your next outing the roles were reversed?
4. If women know men aren't going to stop for directions, why do they ask?
5. Name a time when you "got lost" on a trip with a person of the opposite sex.
6. In the context of women/men relationships, when do you feel powerless? When do you feel adventurous?

CHAPTER 3

1. Discuss the following point: There's a difference between a sanctuary and a hideout. A sanctuary is a place of withdrawing for safety or reflection. A hideout is where we run to avoid conflict or cover our tracks.
2. Name a time when you heard "Honey, I'm going out to _____," and you knew your special someone was

hiding. Did you know what he or she was hiding from? Did you let him or her go?

3. "Why do men tend to hide? Two reasons: 1) We hope not to be found and 2) we hope not to be found out. We're crying out, 'Please don't expose me for who I really am, and for how really incompetent I am.'"

   What are the risks for you to become vulnerable and come out of hiding?

4. How do you feel you have been affected by "hiding" in your relationship(s)?

5. Assignment: Watch the movie *She's Having a Baby*. Where do you see yourself in the characters of Jake and Kristy Briggs?

CHAPTER 4

1. Assignment: Spend an afternoon or evening watching sports with your someone of the opposite sex. Take note of how differently the two of you engage in the experience.

2. Have you ever noticed that when a guy's favorite team loses his mood is more apt to change? Women aren't usually affected as deeply. What's that about?

3. Describe some dreams you have for yourself five, ten, fifteen, and twenty years from now. How do these reflect your core values and needs?

4. Women and men can both be incredibly competitive. What are some differences in how women and men view competition?

5. Where do you most experience adventure and risk in this season of your life?

CHAPTER 5

1. Other than sex . . . list some other things that men can be hasty at when "focused on the prize."
2. Prior to eating the apple, Adam and Eve wandered around the garden *naked* and *shameless*. What do you suppose they did?
3. This chapter describes six common flawed views of sex. These views often occur apart from intercourse and make their way into how women and men relate to each other. Which flawed styles of relating have you experienced?

   Fabrication
   Miscommunication
   Recreation
   Masturbation
   Affirmation
   Compensation

   How might this affect your relationship(s)?

4. Growing up, how did you learn about sex (parents, school, peers, TV, experience, sleepover talk)?
5. At some point, you have experienced sexuality as a shameful event. How have these events affected how you think and feel about sex and your own body?
6. "Sex is worship. Sex is holy. Sex reveals God's glory." What do you experience hearing these statements? Why do some Christians separate sex and God, think sex is dirty and God is clean, and consider sex unholy and God holy?

CHAPTER 6

1. In the vomit story, do you think that Connie's version of the story would be different? If so, how?
2. Assignment: Rent the movie *When Harry Met Sally*. Discuss the differences between Harry and Sally.
3. Discuss this quote from the book: "[Men] get so focused on *finding solutions* that we apply it to every situation, including our relationships. And we believe that the answer is mysteriously hidden in some kind of *action*. We are wired for action. . . . When something goes haywire in our relationships, it exposes our fear of not being enough, of not having what it takes."
4. Describe a time in your life when you were looking for understanding but received advice instead.
5. How do women and men cope with feelings of incompetence and inadequacy? In what ways do we handle it similarly? How are we different?
6. Think back to when you were growing up. How did your mom handle making mistakes and screwing things up? What about your dad? Who are you most like?

CHAPTER 7

1. When you experience conflict, who do you most closely resemble?

   Robin Williams/Tina Fey (comedian)
   Lindsay Lohan/Terrell Owens (drama queen/king)
   Mike Tyson/Courtney Love (rager)

Oprah/Donald Trump (take charge)
Gandhi/Mother Teresa (pacifist)
Paris Hilton/Woody Allen (whiner/childish)
_____ (other)

2. What is the one area of conflict that continues to resurface in your relationship(s)? Who usually wins the fight?
3. Recall the most recent conflict you have had. How would asking the two questions "Is God good?" and "Are we *for* each other?" have changed the outcome of the conflict? Future conflicts?
4. Assignment: Watch the movie *The Story of Us*. Which character(s) do you most closely relate to?
5. In conflict, what are some ways that you . . .

become defensive?
attack the other person?
downplay the issue?
jump ship?

CHAPTER 8

1. Recall a "what were you thinking?" moment, a time when you just couldn't understand what someone of the opposite sex was doing.
2. You could use the term "opposites attract" to mean men and women are attracted to each other. Write down as many "opposites" that describe men and women as come to mind.
3. What continues to confuse you about the opposite sex?
4. How has your awareness of gender and how it plays itself out in relationships changed after reading this book?

5. What is one significant thing you have learned about the other sex through reading this book? How will that change how you operate in your relationships?
6. Where is God pressing you the most in regards to the things you have learned in this book?

NOTES

INTRODUCTION

1. Annalee Newitz, "The Coming Boom," *Wired* (July 2005).

CHAPTER 1: "YUP. NOPE. MAYBE."

1. Deborah Tannen, *You Just Don't Understand: Women and Men in Conversation* (New York: Morrow, 1990).
2. Hara Estroff Marano, "The New Sex Scorecard," *Psychology Today* (Jul/Aug 2003). This article can be viewed at www.psychologytoday.com/articles/pto-20030624-000003&page=1.
3. University of Alberta, "Men and women differ in brain use during same tasks," news release, December 1, 2005.
4. Genesis 1:28, NIV
5. Genesis 2:19-20, NIV
6. See Genesis 1:3-27; John 1:1-3; Romans 4:17.
7. Genesis 2:18, NIV
8. Genesis 2:23, NIV

CHAPTER 2: "I'M NOT LOST."

1. John Eldredge, *Wild at Heart: Discovering the Secret of a Man's Soul* (Nashville: Thomas Nelson, 2001), 5.

CHAPTER 3: "IN A MINUTE."

1. Dr. Barbara Luke and Tamara Eberlein, *When You're Expecting Twins, Triplets, or Quads: A Complete Resource* (New York: Quill, 1999), 11.

2. The dialogue for this section can be found in Genesis 3:9-13.

3. 1 Timothy 5:24-25, NIV

4. Galatians 6:7, TNIV

CHAPTER 4: "CAN'T IT WAIT TILL HALFTIME?"

1. See Genesis 4:1-16

2. Matthew 18:2-6, NIV

3. "Porn in the U.S.A.," CBS News, September 5, 2004. The article can be viewed at www.cbsnews.com/stories/2003/11/21/60minutes/main585049.shtml.

4. "Public Money for Sports Stadiums Can't Be Justified," *Daily Policy Digest,* National Center for Policy Analysis (January 10, 2002).

CHAPTER 5: "WANNA DO IT?"

1. Hara Estroff Marano, "The New Sex Scorecard," *Psychology Today* (Jul/Aug 2003).

2. Primetime Live Poll: American Sex Survey, http://abcnews.go.com/Primetime/PollVault/story?id=156921&page=3. This ABC News "Primetime Live" survey was conducted by telephone, by female interviewers only, August 2–9, 2004, among a random national sample of 1,501 adults. The results have a 2.5-point error margin for all respondents; as in any poll, sampling error is higher for subgroups. Sampling, data collection, and tabulation by TNS of Horsham, PA.

3. See Genesis 1:26-27

4. Genesis 2:24; see also Matthew 19:5; Ephesians 5:31.

5. See Ephesians 5:22-33

6. Genesis 2:24, NIV

CHAPTER 6: "YOUR PROBLEM IS …"

1. Genesis 1:28, NIV
2. Psalm 62:11-12, TNIV
3. Zephaniah 3:17, TNIV
4. See Isaiah 42:13-14
5. See Genesis 3:16-19
6. See Genesis 3:16
7. See Genesis 3:17-19
8. Tony DiCicco and Colleen Hacker with Charles Salzberg, *Catch Them Being Good: Everything You Need to Know to Successfully Coach Girls* (New York: Viking, 2002).

CHAPTER 7: "YOU'RE TOO SENSITIVE!"

1. These statistics can be found at the Center for Disease Control's (CDC) Web site, www.cdc.gov/nchs. National Vital Statistics Report, Vol. 54. No 20. July 21, 2006. Also see the CDC's press release news archives at http://www.cdc.gov/nchs/pressroom/news_archives.htm#Marriage/Divorce
2. Ibid.
3. Center for Disease Control. Cohabitation, Marriage, Divorce, and Remarriage in the United States. Series Report 23, Number 22. 103 pp. (PHS) 98-1998.
4. Ibid.
5. Ibid.
6. "Ka-ching! Wedding price tag nears $30K: Survey: Bridal spending tops $125 billion; parents less likely to foot ballooning bill." May 20, 2005: 4:38 PM EDT. By Grace Wong, CNN/Money staff writer. http://money.cnn.com/2005/05/20/pf/weddings/.

7. Scott M. Stanley and Howard J. Markman, "Marriage in the 90s: A Nationwide Random Phone Survey," a Marital Research Poll by PREP, Inc., Denver, Colorado, May 26, 1997. This article can be viewed online at www.prepinc.com/main/docs/marriage_90s_1997.pdf.

8. John Gottman with Nan Silver, *Why Marriages Succeed or Fail* (New York: Simon & Schuster, 1994).

9. Ibid.

10. Ibid.

11. Anne Moir and David Jessel, *Brain Sex: The Real Difference Between Men and Women* (New York: Carol Publishing Group, 1991).

12. Ibid.

13. Moir and Jessel, 1992, Dell Publishing, New York.

14. Missy Globerman, "Linguist and author lectures on differences in men's and women's conversational styles," *Cornell Chronicle* 28, no. 40 (July 10, 1997).

15. Ibid.

16. *Merriam-Webster's Collegiate Dictionary,* 11th ed., s.v. "tango," "waltz."

17. www.satirpacific.org.

18. Genesis 2:24, NIV

ABOUT THE AUTHORS

Stephen James and David Thomas are coauthors of the companion books *"Does This Dress Make Me Look Fat?"* and *"Yup." "Nope." "Maybe."* (Tyndale), as well as *Becoming a Dad: A Spiritual, Emotional and Practical Guide* (Relevant). Stephen and David are regularly featured on radio and television, including ABC Family Channel's *Living the Life,* and in numerous publications, including *Discipleship Journal* and *Relevant* magazine.

Stephen is the congregational-care pastor at Fellowship Bible Church in Brentwood, Tennessee, and a private-practice counselor. He speaks frequently about men's issues, marriage/relationships, and authentic spirituality. Stephen received his master's in counseling from Mars Hill Graduate School at Western Seminary, Seattle. He and his wife, Heather, live in Nashville with their four children.

David is director of counseling for men and boys at Daystar Counseling Ministries in Nashville. He is the coauthor of *Becoming a Dad: A Spiritual, Emotional and Practical Guide.* He and his wife, Connie, have a daughter and twin sons.